THE l
AND THE UNICORN

SOCIALISM AND
THE ENGLISH GENIUS

By

GEORGE ORWELL

WITH THE INTRODUCTORY ESSAY
Notes on Nationalism

First published in 1941

Read &' Co.

Copyright © 2020 Read & Co. Great Essays

This edition is published by Read & Co. Great Essays,
an imprint of Read & Co.

This book is copyright and may not be reproduced or copied in any
way without the express permission of the publisher in writing.

British Library Cataloguing-in-Publication Data
A catalogue record for this book is available
from the British Library.

Read & Co. is part of Read Books Ltd.
For more information visit
www.readandcobooks.co.uk

CONTENTS

NOTES ON
NATIONALISM

AN INTRODUCTORY ESSAY

1945

Somewhere or other Byron makes use of the French word *longeur*, and remarks in passing that though in England we happen not to have the *word*, we have the *thing* in considerable profusion.

In the same way, there is a habit of mind which is now so widespread that it affects our thinking on nearly every subject, but which has not yet been given a name. As the nearest existing equivalent I have chosen the word 'nationalism', but it will be seen in a moment that I am not using it in quite the ordinary sense, if only because the emotion I am speaking about does not always attach itself to what is called a nation—that is, a single race or a geographical area. It can attach itself to a church or a class, or it may work in a merely negative sense, *against* something or other and without the need for any positive object of loyalty.

By 'nationalism' I mean first of all the habit of assuming that human beings can be classified like insects and that whole blocks of millions or tens of millions of people can be confidently labelled 'good' or 'bad'.[1] But secondly—and this is much more

---

1   Nations, and even vaguer entities such as Catholic Church
     or the proleteriat, are commonly thought of as individuals
     and often referred to as 'she'. Patently absurd remarks such

important—I mean the habit of identifying oneself with a single nation or other unit, placing it beyond good and evil and recognising no other duty than that of advancing its interests. Nationalism is not to be confused with patriotism. Both words are normally used in so vague a way that any definition is liable to be challenged, but one must draw a distinction between them, since two different and even opposing ideas are involved. By 'patriotism' I mean devotion to a particular place and a particular way of life, which one believes to be the best in the world but has no wish to force on other people. Patriotism is of its nature defensive, both militarily and culturally. Nationalism, on the other hand, is inseparable from the desire for power. The abiding purpose of every nationalist is to secure more power and more prestige, *not* for himself but for the nation or other unit in which he has chosen to sink his own individuality.

So long as it is applied merely to the more notorious and identifiable nationalist movements in Germany, Japan, and other countries, all this is obvious enough. Confronted with a phenomenon like Nazism, which we can observe from the outside, nearly all of us would say much the same things about it. But here I must repeat what I said above, that I am only using the word 'nationalism' for lack of a better. Nationalism, in the extended sense in which I am using the word, includes such movements and tendencies as Communism, political Catholicism, Zionism, Antisemitism, Trotskyism and Pacifism. It does not necessarily mean loyalty to a government or a

---

as 'Germany is naturally treacherous' are to be found in any newspaper one opens and reckless generalization about national character ('The Spaniard is a natural aristocrat' or 'Every Englishman is a hypocrite') are uttered by almost everyone. Intermittently these generalizations are seen to be unfounded, but the habit of making them persists, and people of professedly international outlook, e.g., Tolstoy or Bernard Shaw, are often guilty of them.

country, still less to *one's own* country, and it is not even strictly necessary that the units in which it deals should actually exist. To name a few obvious examples, Jewry, Islam, Christendom, the Proletariat and the White Race are all of them objects of passionate nationalistic feeling: but their existence can be seriously questioned, and there is no definition of any one of them that would be universally accepted.

It is also worth emphasising once again that nationalist feeling can be purely negative. There are, for example, Trotskyists who have become simply enemies of the U.S.S.R. without developing a corresponding loyalty to any other unit. When one grasps the implications of this, the nature of what I mean by nationalism becomes a good deal clearer. A nationalist is one who thinks solely, or mainly, in terms of competitive prestige. He may be a positive or a negative nationalist—that is, he may use his mental energy either in boosting or in denigrating—but at any rate his thoughts always turn on victories, defeats, triumphs and humiliations. He sees history, especially contemporary history, as the endless rise and decline of great power units, and every event that happens seems to him a demonstration that his own side is on the upgrade and some hated rival is on the downgrade. But finally, it is important not to confuse nationalism with mere worship of success. The nationalist does not go on the principle of simply ganging up with the strongest side. On the contrary, having picked his side, he persuades himself that it *is* the strongest, and is able to stick to his belief even when the facts are overwhelmingly against him. Nationalism is power-hunger tempered by self-deception. Every nationalist is capable of the most flagrant dishonesty, but he is also—since he is conscious of serving something bigger than himself—unshakeably certain of being in the right.

Now that I have given this lengthy definition, I think it will be admitted that the habit of mind I am talking about is widespread among the English intelligentsia, and more widespread there than among the mass of the people. For those who feel deeply about contemporary politics, certain topics have become so infected by considerations of prestige that a genuinely rational approach to them is almost impossible. Out of the hundreds of examples that one might choose, take this question: Which of the three great allies, the U.S.S.R., Britain and the USA, has contributed most to the defeat of Germany? In theory, it should be possible to give a reasoned and perhaps even a conclusive answer to this question. In practice, however, the necessary calculations cannot be made, because anyone likely to bother his head about such a question would inevitably see it in terms of competitive prestige. He would therefore *start* by deciding in favour of Russia, Britain or America as the case might be, and only *after* this would begin searching for arguments that seemed to support his case. And there are whole strings of kindred questions to which you can only get an honest answer from someone who is indifferent to the whole subject involved, and whose opinion on it is probably worthless in any case. Hence, partly, the remarkable failure in our time of political and military prediction. It is curious to reflect that out of al the 'experts' of all the schools, there was not a single one who was able to foresee so likely an event as the Russo-German Pact of 1939[2]. And when news of the Pact broke, the most wildly divergent explanations were of it were given, and predictions were made which were falsified almost immediately, being based in nearly every case not on a study of probabilities but on a desire to make the U.S.S.R. seem good or bad, strong or weak. Political or military commentators, like astrologers, can survive almost any mistake, because their more devoted followers do not look to them for an appraisal of the facts but

---

2   A few writers of conservative tendency, such as Peter Drucker, foretold an agreement between Germany and Russia, but they expected an actual alliance or amalgamation which would be permanent. No Marxist or other left-wing writer, of whatever colour, came anywhere near foretelling the Pact.

for the stimulation of nationalistic loyalties[3]. And aesthetic judgements, especially literary judgements, are often corrupted in the same way as political ones. It would be difficult for an Indian Nationalist to enjoy reading Kipling or for a Conservative to see merit in Mayakovsky, and there is always a temptation to claim that any book whose tendency one disagrees with must be a bad book from a *literary* point of view. People of strongly nationalistic outlook often perform this sleight of hand without being conscious of dishonesty.

In England, if one simply considers the number of people involved, it is probable that the dominant form of nationalism is old-fashioned British jingoism. It is certain that this is still widespread, and much more so than most observers would have believed a dozen years ago. However, in this essay I am concerned chiefly with the reactions of the intelligentsia, among whom jingoism and even patriotism of the old kind are almost dead, though they now seem to be reviving among a minority. Among the intelligentsia, it hardly needs saying that the dominant form of nationalism is Communism—using this word in a very loose sense, to include not merely Communist

---

3   The military commentators of the popular press can mostly be classified as pro-Russian or anti-Russian pro-blimp or anti-blimp. Such errors as believing the Maginot Line impregnable, or predicting that Russia would conquer Germany in three months, have failed to shake their reputation, because they were always saying what their own particular audience wanted to hear. The two military critics most favoured by the intelligentsia are Captain Liddell Hart and Major-General Fuller, the first of whom teaches that the defence is stronger that the attack, and the second that the attack is stronger that the defence. This contradiction has not prevented both of them from being accepted as authorities by the same public. The secret reason for their vogue in left-wing circles is that both of them are at odds with the War Office.

Party members, but 'fellow travellers' and russophiles generally. A Communist, for my purpose here, is one who looks upon the U.S.S.R. as his Fatherland and feels it his duty t justify Russian policy and advance Russian interests at all costs. Obviously such people abound in England today, and their direct and indirect influence is very great. But many other forms of nationalism also flourish, and it is by noticing the points of resemblance between different and even seemingly opposed currents of thought that one can best get the matter into perspective.

Ten or twenty years ago, the form of nationalism most closely corresponding to Communism today was political Catholicism. Its most outstanding exponent—though he was perhaps an extreme case rather than a typical one—was G. K. Chesterton. Chesterton was a writer of considerable talent who whose to suppress both his sensibilities and his intellectual honesty in the cause of Roman Catholic propaganda. During the last twenty years or so of his life, his entire output was in reality an endless repetition of the same thing, under its laboured cleverness as simple and boring as 'Great is Diana of the Ephesians.' Every book that he wrote, every scrap of dialogue, had to demonstrate beyond the possibility of mistake the superiority of the Catholic over the Protestant or the pagan. But Chesterton was not content to think of this superiority as merely intellectual or spiritual: it had to be translated into terms of national prestige and military power, which entailed an ignorant idealisation of the Latin countries, especially France. Chesterton had not lived long in France, and his picture of it—as a land of Catholic peasants incessantly singing the *Marseillaise* over glasses of red wine—had about as much relation to reality as *chu chin chow* has to everyday life in Baghdad. And with this went not only an enormous overestimation of French military power (both before and after 1914-18 he maintained that France, by itself, was stronger than Germany), but a silly and vulgar glorification of the actual process of war. Chesterton's battle poems, such as Lepanto or The Ballad of Saint Barbara, make The Charge of the Light Brigade read like a pacifist tract: they are perhaps the most tawdry bits of bombast to be found in our language. The interesting thing is that had the romantic rubbish which he habitually wrote about France and the French army been written by somebody else about Britain and the British army, he would have been the first to jeer. In home politics he was a Little Englander, a true hater of jingoism and imperialism, and according to his lights a true friend of democracy. Yet when he looked outwards into the international field, he could forsake his principles without even noticing he was doing so. Thus, his almost mystical belief in the virtues of democracy did not prevent him from admiring Mussolini. Mussolini had destroyed the representative government and the freedom of the press for which Chesterton had struggled so hard at home, but Mussolini was an Italian and had made Italy strong, and that settled the matter. Nor did Chesterton ever find a word to say about imperialism and the conquest of coloured races when they were practised by Italians or Frenchmen. His hold on reality, his literary taste, and even to some extent his moral sense, were dislocated as soon as his nationalistic loyalties were involved.

Obviously there are considerable resemblances between political Catholicism, as exemplified by Chesterton, and Communism. So there are between either of these and for instance Scottish nationalism, Zionism, Antisemitism or Trotskyism. It would be an oversimplification to say that all forms of nationalism are the same, even in their mental atmosphere, but there are certain rules that hold good in all cases. The following are the principal characteristics of nationalist thought:

Obsession. As nearly as possible, no nationalist ever thinks, talks, or writes about anything except the superiority of his own power unit. It is difficult if not impossible for any nationalist to conceal his allegiance. The smallest slur upon his own unit, or any implied praise of a rival organization, fills him with uneasiness which he can relieve only by making some sharp retort. If the chosen unit is an actual country, such as Ireland or India, he will generally claim superiority for it not only in military power and political virtue, but in art, literature, sport, structure of the language, the physical beauty of the inhabitants, and perhaps even in climate, scenery and cooking. He will show great sensitiveness about such things as the correct display of flags, relative size of headlines and the order in which different countries are named[4]. Nomenclature plays a very important part in nationalist thought. Countries which have won their independence or gone through a nationalist revolution usually change their names, and any country or other unit round which strong feelings revolve is likely to have several names, each of them carrying a different implication. The two sides of the Spanish Civil War had between them nine or ten names expressing different degrees of love and hatred. Some of these names (e.g. 'Patriots' for Franco-supporters, or 'Loyalists' for Government-supporters) were frankly question-begging, and there was no single one of the which the two rival factions could have agreed to use. All nationalists consider it a duty to spread their own language to the detriment of rival languages, and among English-speakers this struggle reappears in subtler forms as a struggle between dialects. Anglophobe-Americans will refuse to use a slang phrase if they know it to be of British origin, and the conflict between Latinizers and Germanizers often has nationalists motives behind it. Scottish nationalists insist on the superiority of Lowland Scots, and socialists whose nationalism takes the form of class hatred tirade against the B.B.C. accent and even the often gives the impression of being tinged by belief in sympathetic magic—a belief which probably comes out in the widespread custom of burning political enemies in effigy, or using pictures of them as targets in shooting galleries.

---

4   Certain Americans have expressed dissatisfaction because 'Anglo-American' is the form of combination for these two words. It has been proposed to submit 'Americo-British'.

Instability. The intensity with which they are held does not prevent nationalist loyalties from being transferable. To begin with, as I have pointed out already, they can be and often are fastened up on some foreign country. One quite commonly finds that great national leaders, or the founders of nationalist movements, do not even belong to the country they have glorified. Sometimes they are outright foreigners, or more often they come from peripheral areas where nationality is doubtful. Examples are Stalin, Hitler, Napoleon, de Valera, Disraeli, Poincare, Beaverbrook. The Pan-German movement was in part the creation of an Englishman, Houston Chamberlain. For the past fifty or a hundred years, transferred nationalism has been a common phenomenon among literary intellectuals. With Lafcadio Hearne the transference was to Japan, with Carlyle and many others of his time to Germany, and in our own age it is usually to Russia. But the peculiarly interesting fact is that re-transference is also possible. A country or other unit which has been worshipped for years may suddenly become detestable, and some other object of affection may take its place with almost no interval. In the first version of H. G. Wells's *Outline Of History*, and others of his writings about that time, one finds the United States praised almost as extravagantly as Russia is praised by Communists today: yet within a few years this uncritical admiration had turned into hostility. The bigoted Communist who changes in a space of weeks, or even days, into an equally bigoted Trotskyist is a common spectacle. In continental Europe Fascist movements were largely recruited from among Communists, and the opposite process may well happen within the next few years. What remains constant in the nationalist is his state of mind: the object of his feelings is changeable, and may be imaginary.

But for an intellectual, transference has an important function which I have already mentioned shortly in connection with Chesterton. It makes it possible for him to be much *more* nationalistic—more vulgar, more silly, more malignant, more dishonest—that he could ever be on behalf of his native country, or any unit of which he had real knowledge. When one sees the slavish or boastful rubbish that is written about Stalin, the Red Army, etc. by fairly intelligent and sensitive people, one realises that this is only possible because some kind of dislocation has taken place. In societies such as ours, it is unusual for anyone describable as an intellectual to feel a very deep attachment to his own country. Public opinion—that is, the section of public opinion of which he as an intellectual is aware—will not allow him to do so. Most of the people surrounding him are sceptical and disaffected, and he may adopt the same attitude from imitativeness or sheer cowardice: in that case he will have abandoned the form of nationalism that lies nearest to hand without getting any closer to a genuinely internationalist outlook. He still feels the need for a Fatherland, and it is natural to look for one somewhere abroad. Having found it, he can wallow unrestrainedly in exactly those emotions from which he believes that he has emancipated himself. God, the King, the Empire, the Union Jack—all the overthrown idols can reappear under different names, and because they are not recognised for what they are they can be worshipped with a good conscience. Transferred nationalism, like the use of scapegoats, is a way of attaining salvation without altering one's conduct.

Indifference to Reality. All nationalists have the power of not seeing resemblances between similar sets of facts. A British Tory will defend self-determination in Europe and oppose it in India with no feeling of inconsistency. Actions are held to be good or bad, not on their own merits, but according to who does them, and there is almost no kind of outrage—torture, the use of hostages, forced labour, mass deportations, imprisonment without trial, forgery, assassination, the bombing of civilians—which does not change its moral colour when it is committed by 'our' side. The Liberal *News Chronicle* published, as an example of shocking barbarity, photographs of Russians hanged by the Germans, and then a year or two later published with warm approval almost exactly similar photographs of Germans hanged by the Russians[5]. It is the same with historical events. History is thought of largely in nationalist terms, and such things as the Inquisition, the tortures of the Star Chamber, the exploits of the English buccaneers (Sir Francis Drake, for instance, who was given to sinking Spanish prisoners alive), the Reign of Terror, the heroes of the Mutiny blowing hundreds of Indians from the guns, or Cromwell's soldiers slashing Irishwomen's faces with razors, become morally neutral or even meritorious when it is felt that they were done in the 'right' cause. If one looks back over the past quarter of a century, one finds that there was hardly a single year when atrocity stories were not being reported from some part of the world; and yet in not one single case were these atrocities—in Spain, Russia, China, Hungary, Mexico, Amritsar, Smyrna—believed in and disapproved of by the English intelligentsia as a whole. Whether such deeds were reprehensible, or even whether they happened, was always decided according to political predilection.

The nationalist not only does not disapprove of atrocities committed by his own side, but he has a remarkable capacity for not even hearing about them. For quite six years the English admirers of Hitler contrived not to learn of the existence of Dachau and Buchenwald. And those who are loudest in denouncing the German concentration camps are often quite unaware, or only very dimly aware, that there are also concentration camps in Russia. Huge events like the Ukraine famine of 1933, involving the deaths of millions of people, have actually escaped the attention of the majority of English

5   The *News Chronicle* advised its readers to visit the news film at which the entire execution could be witnessed, with close-ups. The *Star* published with seeming approval photographs of nearly naked female collaborationists being baited by the Paris mob. These photographs had a marked resemblance to the Nazi photographs of Jews being baited by the Berlin mob.

russophiles. Many English people have heard almost nothing about the extermination of German and Polish Jews during the present war. Their own antisemitism has caused this vast crime to bounce off their consciousness. In nationalist thought there are facts which are both true and untrue, known and unknown. A known fact may be so unbearable that it is habitually pushed aside and not allowed to enter into logical processes, or on the other hand it may enter into every calculation and yet never be admitted as a fact, even in one's own mind.

Every nationalist is haunted by the belief that the past can be altered. He spends part of his time in a fantasy world in which things happen as they should—in which, for example, the Spanish Armada was a success or the Russian Revolution was crushed in 1918—and he will transfer fragments of this world to the history books whenever possible. Much of the propagandist writing of our time amounts to plain forgery. Material facts are suppressed, dates altered, quotations removed from their context and doctored so as to change their meaning. Events which it is felt ought not to have happened are left unmentioned and ultimately denied[6]. In 1927 Chiang Kai Shek boiled hundreds of Communists alive, and yet within ten years he had become one of the heroes of the Left. The re-alignment of world politics had brought him into the anti-Fascist camp, and so it was felt that the boiling of the Communists 'didn't count', or perhaps had not happened. The primary aim of propaganda is, of course, to influence contemporary opinion, but those who rewrite history do probably believe with part of their minds that they are actually thrusting facts into the past. When one considers the elaborate forgeries that have been committed in

6   An example is the Russo-German Pact, which is being
     effaced as quickly as possible from public memory. A Russian
     correspondent informs me that mention of the Pact is already
     being omitted from Russian year-books which table recent
     political events.

order to show that Trotsky did not play a valuable part in the Russian civil war, it is difficult to feel that the people responsible are merely lying. More probably they feel that their own version was what happened in the sight of God, and that one is justified in rearranging the records accordingly.

Indifference to objective truth is encouraged by the sealing-off of one part of the world from another, which makes it harder and harder to discover what is actually happening. There can often be a genuine doubt about the most enormous events. For example, it is impossible to calculate within millions, perhaps even tens of millions, the number of deaths caused by the present war. The calamities that are constantly being reported—battles, massacres, famines, revolutions—tend to inspire in the average person a feeling of unreality. One has no way of verifying the facts, one is not even fully certain that they have happened, and one is always presented with totally different interpretations from different sources. What were the rights and wrongs of the Warsaw rising of August 1944? Is it true about the German gas ovens in Poland? Who was really to blame for the Bengal famine? Probably the truth is discoverable, but the facts will be so dishonestly set forth in almost any newspaper that the ordinary reader can be forgiven either for swallowing lies or failing to form an opinion. The general uncertainty as to what is really happening makes it easier to cling to lunatic beliefs. Since nothing is ever quite proved or disproved, the most unmistakable fact can be impudently denied. Moreover, although endlessly brooding on power, victory, defeat, revenge, the nationalist is often somewhat uninterested in what happens in the real world. What he wants is to *feel* that his own unit is getting the better of some other unit, and he can more easily do this by scoring off an adversary than by examining the facts to see whether they support him. All nationalist controversy is at the debating-society level. It is always entirely inconclusive, since each contestant invariably believes himself to have won the victory. Some nationalists are not far from schizophrenia, living quite happily amid dreams of power and conquest which have no connection with the physical world.

I have examined as best as I can the mental habits which are common to all forms of nationalism. The next thing is to classify those forms, but obviously this cannot be done comprehensively. Nationalism is an enormous subject. The world is tormented by innumerable delusions and hatreds which cut across one another in an extremely complex way, and some of the most sinister of them have not yet impinged on the European consciousness. In this essay I am concerned with nationalism as it occurs among the English intelligentsia. In them, much more than in ordinary English people, it is unmixed with patriotism and therefore can be studied pure. Below are listed the varieties of nationalism now flourishing among English intellectuals, with such comments as seem to be needed.

It is convenient to use three headings, Positive, Transferred, and Negative, though some varieties will fit into more than one category:

POSITIVE NATIONALISM

(i) NEO-TORYISM. Exemplified by such people as Lord Elton, A.P. Herbert, G.M. Young, Professor Pickthorn, by the literature of the Tory Reform Committee, and by such magazines as the NEW ENGLISH REVIEW and THE NINETEENTH CENTURY AND AFTER. The real motive force of neo-Toryism, giving it its nationalistic character and differentiating it from ordinary Conservatism, is the desire not to recognise that British power and influence have declined. Even those who are realistic enough to see that Britain's military position is not what it was, tend to claim that 'English ideas' (usually left undefined) must dominate the world. All neo-Tories are anti-Russian, but sometimes the main

18

emphasis is anti-American. The significant thing is that this school of thought seems to be gaining ground among youngish intellectuals, sometimes ex-Communists, who have passed through the usual process of disillusionment and become disillusioned with that. The anglophobe who suddenly becomes violently pro-British is a fairly common figure. Writers who illustrate this tendency are F. A. Voigt, Malcolm Muggeridge, Evelyn Waugh, Hugh Kingsmill, and a psychologically similar development can be observed in T. S. Eliot, Wyndham Lewis, and various of their followers.

(ii) CELTIC NATIONALISM. Welsh, Irish and Scottish nationalism have points of difference but are alike in their anti-English orientation. Members of all three movements have opposed the war while continuing to describe themselves as pro-Russian, and the lunatic fringe has even contrived to be simultaneously pro-Russian and pro-Nazi. But Celtic nationalism is not the same thing as anglophobia. Its motive force is a belief in the past and future greatness of the Celtic peoples, and it has a strong tinge of racialism. The Celt is supposed to be spiritually superior to the Saxon—simpler, more creative, less vulgar, less snobbish, etc.—but the usual power hunger is there under the surface. One symptom of it is the delusion that Eire, Scotland or even Wales could preserve its independence unaided and owes nothing to British protection. Among writers, good examples of this school of thought are Hugh McDiarmid and Sean O'Casey. No modern Irish writer, even of the stature of Yeats or Joyce, is completely free from traces of nationalism.

(iii) ZIONISM. This the unusual characteristics of a nationalist movement, but the American variant of it seems to be more violent and malignant than the British. I classify it under Direct and not Transferred nationalism because it flourishes almost exclusively among the Jews themselves. In England, for several rather incongruous reasons, the intelligentsia are mostly pro-Jew on the Palestine issue, but they do not feel strongly about it. All English people of goodwill are also pro-Jew in the sense of disapproving of Nazi persecution. But any actual nationalistic loyalty, or belief in the innate superiority of Jews, is hardly to be found among Gentiles.

TRANSFERRED NATIONALISM

(i) COMMUNISM.

(ii) POLITICAL CATHOLICISM.

(iii) COLOUR FEELING. The old-style contemptuous attitude towards 'natives' has been much weakened in England, and various pseudo-scientific theories emphasising the superiority of the white race have been abandoned[7]. Among the intelligentsia, colour feeling only occurs in the transposed form, that is, as a belief in the innate superiority of the coloured races. This is now increasingly common among English intellectuals, probably resulting more often from masochism and sexual frustration than from contact with the Oriental and Negro nationalist movements. Even among those who do not feel strongly on the colour question, snobbery and imitation have a powerful influence. Almost any English intellectual would be scandalised by the claim that the white races are superior to the coloured,

---

7   A good example is the sunstroke superstition. Until recently it was believed that the white races were much more liable to sunstroke that the coloured, and that a white man could not safely walk about in tropical sunshine without a pith helmet. There was no evidence whatever for this theory, but it served the purpose of accentuating the difference between 'natives' and Europeans. During the war the theory was quietly dropped and whole armies manoeuvred in the tropics without pith helmets. So long as the sunstroke superstition survived, English doctors in India appear to have believed in it as firmly as laymen.

whereas the opposite claim would seem to him unexceptionable even if he disagreed with it. Nationalistic attachment to the coloured races is usually mixed up with the belief that their sex lives are superior, and there is a large underground mythology about the sexual prowess of Negroes.

(iv) CLASS FEELING. Among upper-class and middle-class intellectuals, only in the transposed form—i.e. as a belief in the superiority of the proletariat. Here again, inside the intelligentsia, the pressure of public opinion is overwhelming. Nationalistic loyalty towards the proletariat, and most vicious theoretical hatred of the bourgeoisie, can and often do co-exist with ordinary snobbishness in everyday life.

(v) PACIFISM. The majority of pacifists either belong to obscure religious sects or are simply humanitarians who object to the taking of life and prefer not to follow their thoughts beyond that point. But there is a minority of intellectual pacifists whose real though unadmitted motive appears to be hatred of western democracy and admiration of totalitarianism. Pacifist propaganda usually boils down to saying that one side is as bad as the other, but if one looks closely at the writings of younger intellectual pacifists, one finds that they do not by any means express impartial disapproval but are directed almost entirely against Britain and the United States. Moreover they do not as a rule condemn violence as such, but only violence used in defence of western countries. The Russians, unlike the British, are not blamed for defending themselves by warlike means, and indeed all pacifist propaganda of this type avoids mention of Russia or China. It is not claimed, again, that the Indians should abjure violence in their struggle against the British. Pacifist literature abounds with equivocal remarks which, if they mean anything, appear to mean that statesmen of the type of Hitler are preferable to those of the type of Churchill, and that violence is perhaps excusable if it is violent enough. After the fall of France, the French pacifists, faced by a real choice which their English colleagues have not had to make, mostly went over to the Nazis, and in England there appears to have been some small overlap of membership between the Peace Pledge Union and the Blackshirts. Pacifist writers have written in praise of Carlyle, one of the intellectual fathers of Fascism. All in all it is difficult not to feel that pacifism, as it appears among a section of the intelligentsia, is secretly inspired by an admiration for power and successful cruelty. The mistake was made of pinning this emotion to Hitler, but it could easily be retransferred.

NEGATIVE NATIONALISM

(i) ANGLOPHOBIA. Within the intelligentsia, a derisive and mildly hostile attitude towards Britain is more or less compulsory, but it is an unfaked emotion in many cases. During the war it was manifested in the defeatism of the intelligentsia, which persisted long after it had become clear that the Axis powers could not win. Many people were undisguisedly pleased when Singapore fell ore when the British were driven out of Greece, and there was a remarkable unwillingness to believe in good news, e.g. el Alamein, or the number of German planes shot down in the Battle of Britain. English left-wing intellectuals did not, of course, actually want the Germans or Japanese to win the war, but many of them could not help getting a certain kick out of seeing their own country humiliated, and wanted to feel that the final victory would be due to Russia, or perhaps America, and not to Britain. In foreign politics many intellectuals follow the principle that any faction backed by Britain must be in the wrong. As a result, 'enlightened' opinion is quite largely a mirror-image of Conservative policy. Anglophobia is always liable to reversal, hence that fairly common spectacle, the pacifist of one war who is a bellicist in the next.

(ii) ANTI-SEMITISM. There is little evidence about this at present, because the Nazi persecutions have made it necessary for any thinking person to side with the Jews against their

22

oppressors. Anyone educated enough to have heard the word 'antisemitism' claims as a matter of course to be free of it, and anti-Jewish remarks are carefully eliminated from all classes of literature. Actually antisemitism appears to be widespread, even among intellectuals, and the general conspiracy of silence probably helps exacerbate it. People of Left opinions are not immune to it, and their attitude is sometimes affected by the fact that Trotskyists and Anarchists tend to be Jews. But antisemitism comes more naturally to people of Conservative tendency, who suspect Jews of weakening national morale and diluting the national culture. Neo-Tories and political Catholics are always liable to succumb to antisemitism, at least intermittently.

(iii) TROTSKYISM. This word is used so loosely as to include Anarchists, democratic Socialists and even Liberals. I use it here to mean a doctrinaire Marxist whose main motive is hostility to the Stalin régime. Trotskyism can be better studied in obscure pamphlets or in papers like the SOCIALIST APPEAL than in the works of Trotsky himself, who was by no means a man of one idea. Although in some places, for instance in the United States, Trotskyism is able to attract a fairly large number of adherents and develop into an organised movement with a petty fuerher of its own, its inspiration is essentially negative. The Trotskyist is AGAINST Stalin just as the Communist is FOR him, and, like the majority of Communists, he wants not so much to alter the external world as to feel that the battle for prestige is going in his own favour. In each case there is the same obsessive fixation on a single subject, the same inability to form a genuinely rational opinion based on probabilities. The fact that Trotskyists are everywhere a persecuted minority, and that the accusation usually made against them, i.e. of collaborating with the Fascists, is obviously false, creates an impression that Trotskyism is intellectually and morally superior to Communism; but it is doubtful whether there is much difference. The most typical Trotskyists, in any case, are ex-Communists, and no one arrives at Trotskyism except via one of the left-wing movements. No

Communist, unless tethered to his party by years of habit, is secure against a sudden lapse into Trotskyism. The opposite process does not seem to happen equally often, though there is no clear reason why it should not.

In the classification I have attempted above, it will seem that I have often exaggerated, oversimplified, made unwarranted assumptions and have left out of account the existence of ordinarily decent motives. This was inevitable, because in this essay I am trying to isolate and identify tendencies which exist in all our minds and pervert our thinking, without necessarily occurring in a pure state or operating continuously. It is important at this point to correct the over-simplified picture which I have been obliged to make. To begin with, one has no right to assume that EVERYONE, or even every intellectual, is infected by nationalism. Secondly, nationalism can be intermittent and limited. An intelligent man may half-succumb to a belief which he knows to be absurd, and he may keep it out of his mind for long periods, only reverting to it in moments of anger or sentimentality, or when he is certain that no important issues are involved. Thirdly, a nationalistic creed may be adopted in good faith from non-nationalistic motives. Fourthly, several kinds of nationalism, even kinds that cancel out, can co-exist in the same person.

All the way through I have said, 'the nationalist does this' or 'the nationalist does that', using for purposes of illustration the extreme, barely sane type of nationalist who has no neutral areas in his mind and no interest in anything except the struggle for power. Actually such people are fairly common, but they are not worth the powder and shot. In real life Lord Elton, D. N. Pritt, Lady Houston, Ezra Pound, Lord Vanisttart, Father Coughlin and all the rest of their dreary tribe have to be fought against, but their intellectual deficiencies hardly need pointing out. Monomania is not interesting, and the fact that no nationalist of the more bigoted kind can write a book which still seems worth reading after a lapse of years has a certain deodorising effect.

But when one has admitted that nationalism has not triumphed everywhere, that there are still peoples whose judgements are not at the mercy of their desires, the fact does remain that the pressing problems—India, Poland, Palestine, the Spanish civil war, the Moscow trials, the American Negroes, the Russo-German Pact or what have you—cannot be, or at least never are, discussed upon a reasonable level. The Eltons and Pritts and Coughlins, each of them simply an enormous mouth bellowing the same lie over and over again, are obviously extreme cases, but we deceive ourselves if we do not realise that we can all resemble them in unguarded moments. Let a certain note be struck, let this or that corn be trodden on—and it may be corn whose very existence has been unsuspected hitherto—and the most fair-minded and sweet-tempered person may suddenly be transformed into a vicious partisan, anxious only to 'score' over his adversary and indifferent as to how many lies he tells or how many logical errors he commits in doing so. When Lloyd George, who was an opponent of the Boer War, announced in the House of Commons that the British communiques, if one added them together, claimed the killing of more Boers than the whole Boer nation contained, it is recorded that Arthur Balfour rose to his feet and shouted 'Cad!' Very few people are proof against lapses of this type. The Negro snubbed by a white woman, the Englishman who hears England ignorantly criticised by an American, the Catholic apologist reminded of the Spanish Armada, will all react in much the same way. One prod to the nerve of nationalism, and the intellectual decencies can vanish, the past can be altered, and the plainest facts can be denied.

If one harbours anywhere in one's mind a nationalistic loyalty or hatred, certain facts, although in a sense known to be true, are inadmissible. Here are just a few examples. I list below five types of nationalist, and against each I append a fact which it is impossible for that type of nationalist to accept, even in his secret thoughts:

BRITISH TORY: Britain will come out of this war with reduced power and prestige.

COMMUNIST: If she had not been aided by Britain and America, Russia would have been defeated by Germany.

IRISH NATIONALIST: Eire can only remain independent because of British protection.

TROTSKYIST: The Stalin régime is accepted by the Russian masses.

PACIFIST: Those who 'abjure' violence can only do so because others are committing violence on their behalf.

All of these facts are grossly obvious if one's emotions do not happen to be involved: but to the kind of person named in each case they are also INTOLERABLE, and so they have to be denied, and false theories constructed upon their denial. I come back to the astonishing failure of military prediction in the present war. It is, I think, true to say that the intelligentsia have been more wrong about the progress of the war than the common people, and that they were more swayed by partisan feelings. The average intellectual of the Left believed, for instance, that the war was lost in 1940, that the Germans were bound to overrun Egypt in 1942, that the Japanese would never be driven out of the lands they had conquered, and that the Anglo-American bombing offensive was making no impression on Germany. He could believe these things because his hatred for the British ruling class forbade him to admit that British plans could succeed. There is no limit to the follies that can be swallowed if one is under the influence of feelings of this kind. I have heard it confidently stated, for instance, that the American troops had been brought to Europe not to fight the Germans but to crush an English revolution. One has to belong to the intelligentsia to believe things like that: no ordinary man could be such a fool. When Hitler invaded Russia, the officials of the MOI issued 'as background' a warning that Russia might be expected to collapse in six weeks. On the other hand the Communists regarded every phase of the war as a Russian victory, even when the Russians were driven back almost to the Caspian Sea and had lost several million prisoners. There is no need to multiply instances. The point is that as soon as fear, hatred, jealousy and power worship are involved, the sense of reality becomes unhinged. And, as I have pointed out already, the sense of right and wrong becomes unhinged also. There is no crime, absolutely none, that cannot be condoned when 'our' side commits it. Even if one does not deny that the crime has happened, even if one knows that it is exactly the same crime as one has condemned in some other case, even if one admits in an intellectual sense that it is unjustified—still one cannot FEEL that it is wrong. Loyalty is involved, and so pity ceases to function.

The reason for the rise and spread of nationalism is far too big a question to be raised here. It is enough to say that, in the forms in which it appears among English intellectuals, it is a distorted reflection of the frightful battles actually happening in the external world, and that its worst follies have been made possible by the breakdown of patriotism and religious belief. If one follows up this train of thought, one is in danger of being led into a species of Conservatism, or into political quietism. It can be plausibly argued, for instance—it is even possibly true—that patriotism is an inoculation against nationalism, that monarchy is a guard against dictatorship, and that organised religion is a guard against superstition. Or again, it can be argued that NO unbiased outlook is possible, that ALL creeds and causes involve the same lies, follies, and barbarities; and this is often advanced as a reason for keeping out of politics altogether. I do not accept this argument, if only because in the modern world no one describable as an intellectual CAN keep out of politics in the sense of not caring about them. I think one must engage in politics—using the word in a wide sense—and that one must have preferences: that is, one must recognise that some causes are objectively better than others, even if they are advanced by equally bad means. As for the nationalistic loves and hatreds that I have spoken of, they are part of the make-up of most of us, whether we like it or not. Whether it is possible to get rid of them I do not know, but I do believe that it is possible to struggle against them, and that this is essentially a MORAL effort. It is a question first of all of discovering what one really is, what one's own feelings really are, and then of making allowance for the inevitable bias. If you hate and fear Russia, if you are jealous of the wealth and power of America, if you despise Jews, if you have a sentiment of inferiority towards the British ruling class, you cannot get rid of those feelings simply by taking thought. But you can at least recognise that you have them, and prevent them from contaminating your mental processes. The emotional urges which are inescapable, and are perhaps even necessary to political action, should be able to exist side by side with an acceptance of reality. But this, I repeat, needs a MORAL effort, and contemporary English literature, so far as it is alive at all to the major issues of our time, shows how few of us are prepared to make it.

PART I

ENGLAND YOUR ENGLAND

I

As I write, highly civilized human beings are flying overhead, trying to kill me.

They do not feel any enmity against me as an individual, nor I against them. They are 'only doing their duty', as the saying goes. Most of them, I have no doubt, are kind-hearted law-abiding men who would never dream of committing murder in private life. On the other hand, if one of them succeeds in blowing me to pieces with a well-placed bomb, he will never sleep any the worse for it. He is serving his country, which has the power to absolve him from evil.

One cannot see the modern world as it is unless one recognizes the overwhelming strength of patriotism, national loyalty. In certain circumstances it can break down, at certain levels of civilization it does not exist, but as a *positive* force there is nothing to set beside it. Christianity and international Socialism are as weak as straw in comparison with it. Hitler and Mussolini rose to power in their own countries very largely because they could grasp this fact and their opponents could not.

Also, one must admit that the divisions between nation and nation are founded on real differences of outlook. Till recently it was thought proper to pretend that all human beings are very much alike, but in fact anyone able to use his eyes knows that the average of human behaviour differs enormously from country to country. Things that could happen in one country could not happen in another. Hitler's June purge, for instance, could not have happened in England. And, as western peoples go, the English are very highly differentiated. There is a sort of back-handed admission of this in the dislike which nearly all foreigners feel for our national way of life. Few Europeans can endure living in England, and even Americans often feel more at home in Europe.

When you come back to England from any foreign country, you have immediately the sensation of breathing a different air. Even in the first few minutes dozens of small things conspire to give you this feeling. The beer is bitterer, the coins are heavier, the grass is greener, the advertisements are more blatant. The crowds in the big towns, with their mild knobby faces, their bad teeth and gentle manners, are different from a European crowd. Then the vastness of England swallows you up, and you lose for a while your feeling that the whole nation has a single identifiable character. Are there really such things as nations? Are we not forty-six million individuals, all different? And the diversity of it, the chaos! The clatter of clogs in the Lancashire mill towns, the to-and-fro of the lorries on the Great North Road, the queues outside the Labour Exchanges, the rattle of pin-tables in the Soho pubs, the old maids hiking to Holy Communion through the mists of the autumn morning—all these are not only fragments, but *characteristic* fragments, of the English scene. How can one make a pattern out of this muddle?

But talk to foreigners, read foreign books or newspapers, and you are brought back to the same thought. Yes, there is something distinctive and recognizable in English civilization. It is a culture as individual as that of Spain. It is somehow bound up with solid breakfasts and gloomy Sundays, smoky towns and winding roads, green fields and red pillar-boxes. It has a flavour of its own. Moreover it is continuous, it stretches into the future and the past, there is something in it that persists, as in a living creature. What can the England of 1940 have in common with the England of 1840? But then, what have you in common with the child of five whose photograph your mother keeps on the mantelpiece? Nothing, except that you happen to be the same person.

And above all, it is *your* civilization, it is you. However much you hate it or laugh at it, you will never be happy away from it for any length of time. The suet puddings and the red pillar-boxes have entered into your soul. Good or evil, it is yours, you belong to it, and this side the grave you will never get away from the marks that it has given you.

Meanwhile England, together with the rest of the world, is changing. And like everything else it can change only in certain directions, which up to a point can be foreseen. That is not to say that the future is fixed, merely that certain alternatives are possible and others not. A seed may grow or not grow, but at any rate a turnip seed never grows into a parsnip. It is therefore of the deepest importance to try and determine what England *is*, before guessing what part England *can play* in the huge events that are happening.

II

National characteristics are not easy to pin down, and when pinned down they often turn out to be trivialities or seem to have no connexion with one another. Spaniards are cruel to animals, Italians can do nothing without making a deafening noise, the Chinese are addicted to gambling. Obviously such things don't matter in themselves. Nevertheless, nothing is causeless, and even the fact that Englishmen have bad teeth can tell something about the realities of English life.

Here are a couple of generalizations about England that would be accepted by almost all observers. One is that the English are not gifted artistically. They are not as musical as the Germans or Italians, painting and sculpture have never flourished in England as they have in France. Another is that, as Europeans go, the English are not intellectual. They have a horror of abstract thought, they feel no need for any philosophy or systematic 'world-view'. Nor is this because they are 'practical', as they are so fond of claiming for themselves. One has only to look at their methods of town planning and water supply, their obstinate clinging to everything that is out of date and a nuisance, a spelling system that defies analysis, and a system of weights and measures that is intelligible only to the compilers of arithmetic books, to see how little they care about mere efficiency. But they have a certain power of acting without taking thought. Their world-famed hypocrisy—their double-faced attitude towards the Empire, for instance—is bound up with this. Also, in moments of supreme crisis the whole nation can suddenly draw together and act upon a species of instinct, really a code of conduct which is understood by almost everyone, though never formulated. The phrase that Hitler coined for the Germans, 'a sleep-walking people', would have been better applied to the English. Not that there is anything to be proud of in being called a sleep-walker.

But here it is worth noting a minor English trait which is extremely well marked though not often commented on, and that is a love of flowers. This is one of the first things that one notices when one reaches England from abroad, especially if one is coming from southern Europe. Does it not contradict the English indifference to the arts? Not really, because it is found in people who have no aesthetic feelings whatever. What it does link up with, however, is another English characteristic which is so much a part of us that we barely notice it, and that is the addiction to hobbies and spare-time occupations, the *privateness* of English life. We are a nation of flower-lovers, but also a nation of stamp-collectors, pigeon-fanciers, amateur carpenters, coupon-snippers, darts-players, crossword-puzzle fans. All the culture that is most truly native centres round things which even when they are communal are not official—

the pub, the football match, the back garden, the fireside and the 'nice cup of tea'. The liberty of the individual is still believed in, almost as in the nineteenth century. But this has nothing to do with economic liberty, the right to exploit others for profit. It is the liberty to have a home of your own, to do what you like in your spare time, to choose your own amusements instead of having them chosen for you from above. The most hateful of all names in an English ear is Nosey Parker. It is obvious, of course, that even this purely private liberty is a lost cause. Like all other modern people, the English are in process of being numbered, labelled, conscripted, 'co-ordinated'. But the pull of their impulses is in the other direction, and the kind of regimentation that can be imposed on them will be modified in consequence. No party rallies, no Youth Movements, no coloured shirts, no Jew-baiting or 'spontaneous' demonstrations. No Gestapo either, in all probability.

But in all societies the common people must live to some extent *against* the existing order. The genuinely popular culture of England is something that goes on beneath the surface, unofficially and more or less frowned on by the authorities. One thing one notices if one looks directly at the common people, especially in the big towns, is that they are not puritanical. They are inveterate gamblers, drink as much beer as their wages will permit, are devoted to bawdy jokes, and use probably the foulest language in the world. They have to satisfy these tastes in the face of astonishing, hypocritical laws (licensing laws, lottery acts, etc. etc.) which are designed to interfere with everybody but in practice allow everything to happen. Also, the common people are without definite religious belief, and have been so for centuries. The Anglican Church never had a real hold on them, it was simply a preserve of the landed gentry, and the Nonconformist sects only influenced minorities. And yet they have retained a deep tinge of Christian feeling, while almost forgetting the name of Christ. The power-worship which is the new religion of Europe, and which has infected the

English intelligentsia, has never touched the common people. They have never caught up with power politics. The 'realism' which is preached in Japanese and Italian newspapers would horrify them. One can learn a good deal about the spirit of England from the comic coloured postcards that you see in the windows of cheap stationers' shops. These things are a sort of diary upon which the English people have unconsciously recorded themselves. Their old-fashioned outlook, their graded snobberies, their mixture of bawdiness and hypocrisy, their extreme gentleness, their deeply moral attitude to life, are all mirrored there.

The gentleness of the English civilization is perhaps its most marked characteristic. You notice it the instant you set foot on English soil. It is a land where the bus conductors are good-tempered and the policemen carry no revolvers. In no country inhabited by white men is it easier to shove people off the pavement. And with this goes something that is always written off by European observers as 'decadence' or hypocrisy, the English hatred of war and militarism. It is rooted deep in history, and it is strong in the lower-middle class as well as the working class. Successive wars have shaken it but not destroyed it. Well within living memory it was common for 'the redcoats' to be booed at in the streets and for the landlords of respectable public houses to refuse to allow soldiers on the premises. In peace time, even when there are two million unemployed, it is difficult to fill the ranks of the tiny standing army, which is officered by the country gentry and a specialized stratum of the middle class, and manned by farm labourers and slum proletarians. The mass of the people are without military knowledge or tradition, and their attitude towards war is invariably defensive. No politician could rise to power by promising them conquests or military 'glory', no Hymn of Hate has ever made any appeal to them. In the last war the songs which the soldiers made up and sang of their own accord were not vengeful but humorous and mock-defeatist[1]. The only enemy they ever named was the sergeant-major.

In England all the boasting and flag-wagging, the 'Rule Britannia' stuff, is done by small minorities. The patriotism of the common people is not vocal or even conscious. They do not retain among their historical memories the name of a single military victory. English literature, like other literatures, is full of battle-poems, but it is worth noticing that the ones that have won for themselves a kind of popularity are always a tale of disasters and retreats. There is no popular poem about Trafalgar or Waterloo, for instance. Sir John Moore's army at Corunna, fighting a desperate rearguard action before escaping overseas (just like Dunkirk!) has more appeal than a brilliant victory. The most stirring battle-poem in English is about a brigade of cavalry which charged in the wrong direction. And of the last war, the four names which have really engraved themselves on the popular memory are Mons, Ypres, Gallipoli and Passchendaele, every time a disaster. The names of the great battles that finally broke the German armies are simply unknown to the general public.

The reason why the English anti-militarism disgusts foreign observers is that it ignores the existence of the British Empire. It looks like sheer hypocrisy. After all, the English have absorbed a quarter of the earth and held on to it by means of a huge navy. How dare they then turn round and say that war is wicked?

---

1   For example:

> 'I don't want to join the bloody Army,
> I don't want to go unto the war;
> I want no more to roam,
> I'd rather stay at home,
> Living on the earnings of a whore.

But it was not in that spirit that they fought.

It is quite true that the English are hypocritical about their Empire. In the working class this hypocrisy takes the form of not knowing that the Empire exists. But their dislike of standing armies is a perfectly sound instinct. A navy employs comparatively few people, and it is an external weapon which cannot affect home politics directly. Military dictatorships exist everywhere, but there is no such thing as a naval dictatorship. What English people of nearly all classes loathe from the bottom of their hearts is the swaggering officer type, the jingle of spurs and the crash of boots. Decades before Hitler was ever heard of, the word 'Prussian' had much the same significance in England as 'Nazi' has today. So deep does this feeling go that for a hundred years past the officers of the British army, in peace time, have always worn civilian clothes when off duty.

One rapid but fairly sure guide to the social atmosphere of a country is the parade-step of its army. A military parade is really a kind of ritual dance, something like a ballet, expressing a certain philosophy of life. The goose-step, for instance, is one of the most horrible sights in the world, far more terrifying than a dive-bomber. It is simply an affirmation of naked power; contained in it, quite consciously and intentionally, is the vision of a boot crashing down on a face. Its ugliness is part of its essence, for what it is saying is 'Yes, I am *ugly*, and you daren't laugh at me', like the bully who makes faces at his victim. Why is the goose-step not used in England? There are, heaven knows, plenty of army officers who would be only too glad to introduce some such thing. It is not used because the people in the street would laugh. Beyond a certain point, military display is only possible in countries where the common people dare not laugh at the army. The Italians adopted the goose-step at about the time when Italy passed definitely under German control, and, as one would expect, they do it less well than the Germans. The Vichy government, if it survives, is bound to introduce a stiffer parade-ground discipline into what is left of the French army. In the British army the drill is rigid and complicated, full of memories of the eighteenth century, but without definite swagger; the march is merely a formalized walk. It belongs to a society which is ruled by the sword, no doubt, but a sword which must never be taken out of the scabbard.

And yet the gentleness of English civilization is mixed up with barbarities and anachronisms. Our criminal law is as out-of-date as the muskets in the Tower. Over against the Nazi Storm Trooper you have got to set that typically English figure, the hanging judge, some gouty old bully with his mind rooted in the nineteenth century, handing out savage sentences. In England people are still hanged by the neck and flogged with the cat o' nine tails. Both of these punishments are obscene as well as cruel, but there has never been any genuinely popular outcry against them. People accept them (and Dartmoor, and Borstal) almost as they accept the weather. They are part of 'the law', which is assumed to be unalterable.

Here one comes upon an all-important English trait: the respect for constitutionalism and legality, the belief in 'the law' as something above the State and above the individual, something which is cruel and stupid, of course, but at any rate *incorruptible*.

It is not that anyone imagines the law to be just. Everyone knows that there is one law for the rich and another for the poor. But no one accepts the implications of this, everyone takes it for granted that the law, such as it is, will be respected, and feels a sense of outrage when it is not. Remarks like 'They can't run me in; I haven't done anything wrong', or 'They can't do that; it's against the law', are part of the atmosphere of England. The professed enemies of society have this feeling as strongly as anyone else. One sees it in prison-books like Wilfred Macartney's *Walls Have Mouths* or Jim Phelan's *Jail Journey*, in the solemn idiocies that take place at the trials of conscientious objectors, in letters to the papers from eminent Marxist professors, pointing out that this or that is a 'miscarriage of British justice'. Everyone believes in his heart that the law can be, ought to be, and, on the whole, will be impartially administered. The totalitarian idea that there is no such thing as law, there is only power, has never taken root. Even the intelligentsia have only accepted it in theory.

An illusion can become a half-truth, a mask can alter the expression of a face. The familiar arguments to the effect that democracy is 'just the same as' or 'just as bad as' totalitarianism never take account of this fact. All such arguments boil down to saying that half a loaf is the same as no bread. In England such concepts as justice, liberty and objective truth are still believed in. They may be illusions, but they are very powerful illusions. The belief in them influences conduct, national life is different because of them. In proof of which, look about you. Where are the rubber truncheons, where is the castor oil? The sword is still in the scabbard, and while it stays there corruption cannot go beyond a certain point. The English electoral system, for instance, is an all but open fraud. In a dozen obvious ways it is gerrymandered in the interest of the moneyed class. But until some deep change has occurred in the public mind, it cannot become *completely* corrupt. You do not arrive at the polling booth to find men with revolvers telling you which way to vote, nor are the votes miscounted, nor is there any direct bribery. Even hypocrisy is a powerful safeguard. The hanging judge, that evil old man in scarlet robe and horse-hair wig, whom nothing short of dynamite will ever teach what century he is living in, but who will at any rate interpret the law according to the books and will in no circumstances take a money bribe, is one of the symbolic figures of England. He is a symbol of the strange mixture of reality and illusion, democracy and privilege, humbug and decency, the subtle network of compromises, by which the nation keeps itself in its familiar shape.

III

I have spoken all the while of 'the nation', 'England', 'Britain', as though forty-five million souls could somehow be treated as a unit. But is not England notoriously two nations, the rich and the poor? Dare one pretend that there is anything in common between people with £100,000 a year and people with £1 a week? And even Welsh and Scottish readers are likely to have been offended because I have used the word 'England' oftener than 'Britain', as though the whole population dwelt in London and the Home Counties and neither north nor west possessed a culture of its own.

One gets a better view of this question if one considers the minor point first. It is quite true that the so-called races of Britain feel themselves to be very different from one another. A Scotsman, for instance, does not thank you if you call him an Englishman. You can see the hesitation we feel on this point by the fact that we call our islands by no less than six different names, England, Britain, Great Britain, the British Isles, the United Kingdom and, in very exalted moments, Albion. Even the differences between north and south England loom large in our own eyes. But somehow these differences fade away the moment that any two Britons are confronted by a European. It is very rare to meet a foreigner, other than an American, who can distinguish between English and Scots or even English and Irish. To a Frenchman, the Breton and the Auvergnat seem very different beings, and the accent of Marseilles is a stock joke in Paris. Yet we speak of 'France' and 'the French', recognizing France as an entity, a single civilization, which in fact it is. So also with ourselves. Looked at from the outsider even the cockney and the Yorkshireman have a strong family resemblance.

And even the distinction between rich and poor dwindles somewhat when one regards the nation from the outside. There is no question about the inequality of wealth in England. It is grosser than in any European country, and you have only to look down the nearest street to see it. Economically, England is certainly two nations, if not three or four. But at the same time the vast majority of the people *feel* themselves to be a single nation and are conscious of resembling one another more than they resemble foreigners. Patriotism is usually stronger than class-hatred, and always stronger than any kind of internationalism. Except for a brief moment in 1920 (the 'Hands off Russia' movement) the British working class have never thought or acted internationally. For two and a half years they watched their comrades in Spain slowly strangled, and never aided them by even a single strike[2]. But when their own country (the country of Lord Nuffield and Mr Montagu Norman) was in danger, their attitude was very different. At the moment when it seemed likely that England might be invaded, Anthony Eden appealed over the radio for Local Defence Volunteers. He got a quarter of a million men in the first twenty-four hours, and another million in the subsequent month. One has only to compare these figures with, for instance, the number of conscientious objectors to see how vast is the strength of traditional loyalties compared with new ones.

In England patriotism takes different forms in different classes, but it runs like a connecting thread through nearly all of them. Only the Europeanized intelligentsia are really immune to it. As a positive emotion it is stronger in the middle class than in the upper class—the cheap public schools, for instance, are more given to patriotic demonstrations than the expensive ones—but the number of definitely treacherous rich men, the Laval-Quisling type, is probably very small. In the working class patriotism is profound, but it is unconscious. The working man's heart does not leap when he sees a Union Jack. But the famous

---

2   It is true that they aided them to a certain extent with money. Still, the sums raised for the various aid-Spain funds would not equal five per cent of the turnover of the football pools during the same period.

'insularity' and 'xenophobia' of the English is far stronger in the working class than in the bourgeoisie. In all countries the poor are more national than the rich, but the English working class are outstanding in their abhorrence of foreign habits. Even when they are obliged to live abroad for years they refuse either to accustom themselves to foreign food or to learn foreign languages. Nearly every Englishman of working-class origin considers it effeminate to pronounce a foreign word correctly. During the war of 1914-18 the English working class were in contact with foreigners to an extent that is rarely possible. The sole result was that they brought back a hatred of all Europeans, except the Germans, whose courage they admired. In four years on French soil they did not even acquire a liking for wine. The insularity of the English, their refusal to take foreigners seriously, is a folly that has to be paid for very heavily from time to time. But it plays its part in the English mystique, and the intellectuals who have tried to break it down have generally done more harm than good. At bottom it is the same quality in the English character that repels the tourist and keeps out the invader.

Here one comes back to two English characteristics that I pointed out, seemingly at random, at the beginning of the last chapter. One is the lack of artistic ability. This is perhaps another way of saying that the English are outside the European culture. For there is one art in which they have shown plenty of talent, namely literature. But this is also the only art that cannot cross frontiers. Literature, especially poetry, and lyric poetry most of all, is a kind of family joke, with little or no value outside its own language-group. Except for Shakespeare, the best English poets are barely known in Europe, even as names. The only poets who are widely read are Byron, who is admired for the wrong reasons, and Oscar Wilde, who is pitied as a victim of English hypocrisy. And linked up with this, though not very obviously, is the lack of philosophical faculty, the absence in nearly all Englishmen of any need for an ordered system of thought or even for the use of logic.

Up to a point, the sense of national unity is a substitute for a 'world-view'. Just because patriotism is all but universal and not even the rich are uninfluenced by it, there can be moments when the whole nation suddenly swings together and does the same thing, like a herd of cattle facing a wolf. There was such a moment, unmistakably, at the time of the disaster in France. After eight months of vaguely wondering what the war was about, the people suddenly knew what they had got to do: first, to get the army away from Dunkirk, and secondly to prevent invasion. It was like the awakening of a giant. Quick! Danger! The Philistines be upon thee, Samson! And then the swift unanimous action—and, then, alas, the prompt relapse into sleep. In a divided nation that would have been exactly the moment for a big peace movement to arise. But does this mean that the instinct of the English will always tell them to do the right thing? Not at all, merely that it will tell them to do the same thing. In the 1931 General Election, for instance, we all did the wrong thing in perfect unison. We were as single-minded as the Gadarene swine. But I honestly doubt whether we can say that we were shoved down the slope against our will.

It follows that British democracy is less of a fraud than it sometimes appears. A foreign observer sees only the huge inequality of wealth, the unfair electoral system, the governing-class control over the press, the radio and education, and concludes that democracy is simply a polite name for dictatorship. But this ignores the considerable agreement that does unfortunately exist between the leaders and the led. However much one may hate to admit it, it is almost certain that between 1931 and 1940 the National Government represented the will of the mass of the people. It tolerated slums, unemployment and a cowardly foreign policy. Yes, but so did public opinion. It was a stagnant period, and its natural leaders were mediocrities.

In spite of the campaigns of a few thousand left-wingers, it is fairly certain that the bulk of the English people were behind Chamberlain's foreign policy. More, it is fairly certain that the same struggle was going on in Chamberlain's mind as in the minds of ordinary people. His opponents professed to see in him a dark and wily schemer, plotting to sell England to Hitler, but it is far likelier that he was merely a stupid old man doing his best according to his very dim lights. It is difficult otherwise to explain the contradictions of his policy, his failure to grasp any of the courses that were open to him. Like the mass of the people, he did not want to pay the price either of peace or of war. And public opinion was behind him all the while, in policies that were completely incompatible with one another. It was behind him when he went to Munich, when he tried to come to an understanding with Russia, when he gave the guarantee to Poland, when he honoured it, and when he prosecuted the war half-heartedly. Only when the results of his policy became apparent did it turn against him; which is to say that it turned against its own lethargy of the past seven years. Thereupon the people picked a leader nearer to their mood, Churchill, who was at any rate able to grasp that wars are not won without fighting. Later, perhaps, they will pick another leader who can grasp that only Socialist nations can fight effectively.

Do I mean by all this that England is a genuine democracy? No, not even a reader of the *Daily Telegraph* could quite swallow that.

England is the most class-ridden country under the sun. It is a land of snobbery and privilege, ruled largely by the old and silly. But in any calculation about it one has got to take into account its emotional unity, the tendency of nearly all its inhabitants to feel alike and act together in moments of supreme crisis. It is the only great country in Europe that is not obliged to drive hundreds of thousands of its nationals into exile or the concentration camp. At this moment, after a year of war, newspapers and pamphlets abusing the Government, praising the enemy and clamouring for surrender are being sold on the streets, almost without interference. And this is less from a respect for freedom of speech than from a simple perception that these things don't matter. It is safe to let a paper like *Peace News* be sold, because it is certain that ninety-five per cent of the population will never want to read it. The nation is bound together by an invisible chain. At any normal time the ruling class will rob, mismanage, sabotage, lead us into the muck; but let popular opinion really make itself heard, let them get a tug from below that they cannot avoid feeling, and it is difficult for them not to respond. The left-wing writers who denounce the whole of the ruling class as 'pro-Fascist' are grossly over-simplifying. Even among the inner clique of politicians who brought us to our present pass, it is doubtful whether there were any *conscious* traitors. The corruption that happens in England is seldom of that kind. Nearly always it is more in the nature of self-deception, of the right hand not knowing what the left hand doeth. And being unconscious, it is limited. One sees this at its most obvious in the English press. Is the English press honest or dishonest? At normal times it is deeply dishonest. All the papers that matter live off their advertisements, and the advertisers exercise an indirect censorship over news. Yet I do not suppose there is one paper in England that can be straightforwardly bribed with hard cash. In the France of the Third Republic all but a very few of the newspapers could notoriously be bought over the counter like so many pounds of cheese. Public life in England has never been *openly* scandalous. It has not reached the pitch of disintegration at which humbug can be dropped.

England is not the jewelled isle of Shakespeare's much-quoted message, nor is it the inferno depicted by Dr Goebbels. More than either it resembles a family, a rather stuffy Victorian family, with not many black sheep in it but with all its cupboards bursting with skeletons. It has rich relations who have to be kow-towed to and poor relations who are horribly sat upon, and there is a deep conspiracy of silence about the source of the family income. It is a family in which the young are generally thwarted and most of the power is in the hands of irresponsible uncles and bedridden aunts. Still, it is a family. It has its private language and its common memories, and at the approach of an enemy it closes its ranks. A family with the wrong members in control—that, perhaps, is as near as one can come to describing England in a phrase.

IV

Probably the battle of Waterloo was won on the playing-fields of Eton, but the opening battles of all subsequent wars have been lost there. One of the dominant facts in English life during the past three quarters of a century has been the decay of ability in the ruling class.

In the years between 1920 and 1940 it was happening with the speed of a chemical reaction. Yet at the moment of writing it is still possible to speak of a ruling class. Like the knife which has had two new blades and three new handles, the upper fringe of English society is still almost what it was in the mid nineteenth century. After 1832 the old land-owning aristocracy steadily lost power, but instead of disappearing or becoming a fossil they simply intermarried with the merchants, manufacturers and financiers who had replaced them, and soon turned them into accurate copies of themselves. The wealthy ship owner or cotton-miller set up for himself an alibi as a country gentleman, while his sons learned the right mannerisms at public schools which had been designed for just that purpose. England was ruled by an aristocracy constantly recruited from parvenus. And considering what energy the self-made men possessed, and considering that they were buying their way into a class which at any rate had a tradition of public service, one might have expected that able rulers could be produced in some such way.

And yet somehow the ruling class decayed, lost its ability, its daring, finally even its ruthlessness, until a time came when stuffed shirts like Eden or Halifax could stand out as men of exceptional talent. As for Baldwin, one could not even dignify him with the name of stuffed shirt. He was simply a hole in the air. The mishandling of England's domestic problems during the nineteen-twenties had been bad enough, but British foreign policy between 1931 and 1939 is one of the wonders of the world. Why? What had happened? What was it that at every decisive moment made every British statesman do the wrong thing with so unerring an instinct?

The underlying fact was that the whole position of the moneyed class had long ceased to be justifiable. There they sat, at the centre of a vast empire and a world-wide financial network, drawing interest and profits and spending them— on what? It was fair to say that life within the British Empire was in many ways better than life outside it. Still, the Empire was underdeveloped, India slept in the Middle Ages, the Dominions lay empty, with foreigners jealously barred out, and even England was full of slums and unemployment. Only half a million people, the people in the country houses, definitely benefited from the existing system. Moreover, the tendency of small businesses to merge together into large ones robbed more and more of the moneyed class of their function and turned them into mere owners, their work being done for them by salaried managers and technicians. For long past there had been in England an entirely functionless class, living on money that was invested they hardly knew where, the 'idle rich', the people whose photographs you can look at in the *Tatler* and the *Bystander*, always supposing that you want to. The existence of these people was by any standard unjustifiable. They were simply parasites, less useful to society than his fleas are to a dog.

By 1920 there were many people who were aware of all this. By 1930 millions were aware of it. But the British ruling class obviously could not admit to themselves that their usefulness was at an end. Had they done that they would have had to abdicate. For it was not possible for them to turn themselves into mere bandits, like the American millionaires, consciously clinging to unjust privileges and beating down opposition by bribery and tear-gas bombs. After all, they belonged to a class with a certain tradition, they had been to public schools where the duty of dying for your country, if necessary, is laid down as the first and greatest of the Commandments. They had to *feel* themselves true patriots, even while they plundered their countrymen. Clearly there was only one escape for them—into stupidity. They could keep society in its existing shape only by being *unable* to grasp that any improvement was possible. Difficult though this was, they achieved it, largely by fixing their eyes on the past and refusing to notice the changes that were going on round them.

There is much in England that this explains. It explains the decay of country life, due to the keeping-up of a sham feudalism which drives the more spirited workers off the land. It explains the immobility of the public schools, which have barely altered since the eighties of the last century. It explains the military incompetence which has again and again startled the world. Since the fifties every war in which England has engaged has started off with a series of disasters, after which the situation has been saved by people comparatively low in the social scale. The higher commanders, drawn from the aristocracy, could never prepare for modern war, because in order to do so they would have had to admit to themselves that the world was changing. They have always clung to obsolete methods and weapons, because they inevitably saw each war as a repetition of the last. Before the Boer War they prepared for the Zulu War, before the 1914 for the Boer War, and before the present war for 1914. Even at this moment hundreds of thousands of men in England are being trained with the bayonet, a weapon entirely useless except for opening tins. It is worth noticing that the navy and, latterly, the air force, have always been more efficient than the regular army. But the navy is only partially, and the air force hardly at all, within the ruling-class orbit.

It must be admitted that so long as things were peaceful the methods of the British ruling class served them well enough. Their own people manifestly tolerated them. However unjustly England might be organized, it was at any rate not torn by class warfare or haunted by secret police. The Empire was peaceful as no area of comparable size has ever been. Throughout its vast extent, nearly a quarter of the earth, there were fewer armed men than would be found necessary by a minor Balkan state. As people to live under, and looking at them merely from a liberal, *negative* standpoint, the British ruling class had their points. They were preferable to the truly modern men, the Nazis and Fascists. But it had long been obvious that they would be helpless against any serious attack from the outside.

They could not struggle against Nazism or Fascism, because they could not understand them. Neither could they have struggled against Communism, if Communism had been a serious force in western Europe. To understand Fascism they would have had to study the theory of Socialism, which would have forced them to realize that the economic system by which they lived was unjust, inefficient and out-of-date. But it was exactly this fact that they had trained themselves never to face. They dealt with Fascism as the cavalry generals of 1914 dealt with the machine-guns—by ignoring it. After years of aggression and massacres, they had grasped only one fact, that Hitler and Mussolini were hostile to Communism. Therefore, it was argued, they *must* be friendly to the British dividend-drawer. Hence the truly frightening spectacle of Conservative M.P.s wildly cheering the news that British ships, bringing food to the Spanish Republican government, had been bombed by Italian aeroplanes. Even when they had begun to grasp that Fascism was dangerous, its essentially revolutionary nature, the huge military effort it was capable of making, the sort of tactics it would use, were quite beyond their comprehension. At the time of the Spanish Civil War, anyone with as much political knowledge as can be acquired from a sixpenny pamphlet on Socialism knew that, if Franco won, the result would be strategically disastrous for England; and yet generals and admirals who had given their lives to the study of war were unable to grasp this fact. This vein of political ignorance runs right through English official life, through Cabinet ministers, ambassadors, consuls, judges, magistrates, policemen. The policeman who arrests the 'red' does not understand the theories the 'red' is preaching; if he did his own position as bodyguard of the moneyed class might seem less pleasant to him. There is reason to think that even military espionage is hopelessly hampered by ignorance of the new economic doctrines and the ramifications of the underground parties.

The British ruling class were not altogether wrong in thinking that Fascism was on their side. It is a fact that any rich man, unless he is a Jew, has less to fear from Fascism than from either Communism or democratic Socialism. One ought never to forget this, for nearly the whole of German and Italian propaganda is designed to cover it up. The natural instinct of men like Simon, Hoare, Chamberlain etc. was to come to an agreement with Hitler. But—and here the peculiar feature of English life that I have spoken of, the deep sense of national solidarity, comes in— they could only do so by breaking up the Empire and selling their own people into semi-slavery. A truly corrupt class would have done this without hesitation, as in France. But things had not gone that distance in England. Politicians who would make cringing speeches about 'the duty of loyalty to our conquerors' are hardly to be found in English public life. Tossed to and fro between their incomes and their principles, it was impossible that men like Chamberlain should do anything but make the worst of both worlds.

One thing that has always shown that the English ruling class are *morally* fairly sound, is that in time of war they are ready enough to get themselves killed. Several dukes, earls and what nots were killed in the recent campaign in Flanders. That could not happen if these people were the cynical scoundrels that they are sometimes declared to be. It is important not to misunderstand their motives, or one cannot predict their actions. What is to be expected of them is not treachery, or physical cowardice, but stupidity, unconscious sabotage, an infallible instinct for doing the wrong thing. They are not wicked, or not altogether wicked; they are merely unteachable. Only when their money and power are gone will the younger among them begin to grasp what century they are living in.

V

The stagnation of the Empire in the between-war years affected everyone in England, but it had an especially direct effect upon two important sub-sections of the middle class. One was the military and imperialist middle class, generally nicknamed the Blimps, and the other the left-wing intelligentsia. These two seemingly hostile types, symbolic opposites—the half-pay colonel with his bull neck and diminutive brain, like a dinosaur, the highbrow with his domed forehead and stalk-like neck—are mentally linked together and constantly interact upon one another; in any case they are born to a considerable extent into the same families.

Thirty years ago the Blimp class was already losing its vitality. The middle-class families celebrated by Kipling, the prolific lowbrow families whose sons officered the army and navy and swarmed over all the waste places of the earth from the Yukon to the Irrawaddy, were dwindling before 1914. The thing that had killed them was the telegraph. In a narrowing world, more and more governed from Whitehall, there was every year less room for individual initiative. Men like Clive, Nelson, Nicholson, Gordon would find no place for themselves in the modern British Empire. By 1920 nearly every inch of the colonial empire was in the grip of Whitehall. Well-meaning, over-civilized men, in dark suits and black felt hats, with neatly rolled umbrellas crooked over the left forearm, were imposing their constipated view of life on Malaya and Nigeria, Mombasa and Mandalay. The one-time empire builders were reduced to the status of clerks, buried deeper and deeper under mounds of paper and red tape. In the early twenties one could see, all over the Empire, the older officials, who had known more spacious days, writhing impotently under the changes that were happening. From that time onwards it has been next door to impossible to induce young men of spirit to take any part in imperial administration. And what was true of the official world was true also of the commercial. The great monopoly companies swallowed up hosts of petty traders. Instead of going out to trade adventurously in the Indies one went to an office stool in Bombay or Singapore. And life in Bombay or Singapore was actually duller and safer than life in London. Imperialist sentiment remained strong in the middle class, chiefly owing to family tradition, but the job of administering the Empire had ceased to appeal. Few able men went east of Suez if there was any way of avoiding it.

But the general weakening of imperialism, and to some extent of the whole British morale, that took place during the nineteen-thirties, was partly the work of the left-wing intelligentsia, itself a kind of growth that had sprouted from the stagnation of the Empire.

It should be noted that there is now no intelligentsia that is not in some sense 'left'. Perhaps the last right-wing intellectual was T. E. Lawrence. Since about 1930 everyone describable as an 'intellectual' has lived in a state of chronic discontent with the existing order. Necessarily so, because society as it was constituted had no room for him. In an Empire that was simply stagnant, neither being developed nor falling to pieces, and in an England ruled by people whose chief asset was their stupidity, to be 'clever' was to be suspect. If you had the kind of brain that could understand the poems of T. S. Eliot or the theories of Karl Marx, the higher-ups would see to it that you were kept out of any important job. The intellectuals could find a function for themselves only in the literary reviews and the left-wing political parties.

The mentality of the English left-wing intelligentsia can be studied in half a dozen weekly and monthly papers. The immediately striking thing about all these papers is their generally negative, querulous attitude, their complete lack at all times of any constructive suggestion. There is little in them except the irresponsible carping of people who have never been and never expect to be in a position of power. Another marked characteristic is the emotional shallowness of people who live in a world of ideas and have little contact with physical reality. Many intellectuals of the Left were flabbily pacifist up to 1935, shrieked for war against Germany in the years 1935-9, and then promptly cooled off when the war started. It is broadly though not precisely true that the people who were most 'anti-Fascist' during the Spanish Civil War are most defeatist now. And underlying this is the really important fact about so many of the English intelligentsia—their severance from the common culture of the country.

In intention, at any rate, the English intelligentsia are Europeanized. They take their cookery from Paris and their opinions from Moscow. In the general patriotism of the country they form a sort of island of dissident thought. England is perhaps the only great country whose intellectuals are ashamed of their own nationality. In left-wing circles it is always felt that there is something slightly disgraceful in being an Englishman and that it is a duty to snigger at every English institution, from horse racing to suet puddings. It is a strange fact, but it is unquestionably true that almost any English intellectual would feel more ashamed of standing to attention during 'God save the King' than of stealing from a poor box. All through the critical years many left-wingers were chipping away at English morale, trying to spread an outlook that was sometimes squashily pacifist, sometimes violently pro-Russian, but always anti-British. It is questionable how much effect this had, but it certainly had some. If the English people suffered for several years a real weakening of morale, so that the Fascist nations judged that they were 'decadent' and that it was safe to plunge into war, the intellectual sabotage from the Left was partly responsible. Both the *New Statesman* and the *News Chronicle* cried out against the Munich settlement, but even they had done something to make it possible. Ten years of systematic Blimp-baiting affected even the Blimps themselves and made it harder than it had been before to get intelligent young men to enter the armed forces. Given the stagnation of the Empire, the military middle class must have decayed in any case, but the spread of a shallow Leftism hastened the process.

It is clear that the special position of the English intellectuals during the past ten years, as purely *negative* creatures, mere anti-Blimps, was a by-product of ruling-class stupidity. Society could not use them, and they had not got it in them to see that devotion to one's country implies 'for better, for worse'. Both Blimps and highbrows took for granted, as though it were a law of nature, the divorce between patriotism and intelligence. If you were a patriot you read *Blackwood's Magazine* and publicly thanked God that you were 'not brainy'. If you were an intellectual you sniggered at the Union Jack and regarded physical courage as barbarous. It is obvious that this preposterous convention cannot continue. The Bloomsbury highbrow, with his mechanical snigger, is as out-of-date as the cavalry colonel. A modern nation cannot afford either of them. Patriotism and intelligence will have to come together again. It is the fact that we are fighting a war, and a very peculiar kind of war, that may make this possible.

VI

One of the most important developments in England during the past twenty years has been the upward and downward extension of the middle class. It has happened on such a scale as to make the old classification of society into capitalists, proletarians and petit bourgeois (small property-owners) almost obsolete.

England is a country in which property and financial power are concentrated in very few hands. Few people in modern England *own* anything at all, except clothes, furniture and possibly a house. The peasantry have long since disappeared, the independent shopkeeper is being destroyed, the small businessman is diminishing in numbers. But at the same time modern industry is so complicated that it cannot get along without great numbers of managers, salesmen, engineers, chemists and technicians of all kinds, drawing fairly large salaries. And these in turn call into being a professional class of doctors, lawyers, teachers, artists, etc. etc. The tendency of advanced capitalism has therefore been to enlarge the middle class and not to wipe it out as it once seemed likely to do.

But much more important than this is the spread of middle-class ideas and habits among the working class. The British working class are now better off in almost all ways than they were thirty years ago. This is partly due to the efforts of the trade unions, but partly to the mere advance of physical science. It is not always realized that within rather narrow limits the standard of life of a country can rise without a corresponding rise in real wages. Up to a point, civilization can lift itself up by its boot-tags. However unjustly society is organized, certain technical advances are bound to benefit the whole community, because certain kinds of goods are necessarily held in common. A millionaire cannot, for example, light the streets for himself while darkening them for other people. Nearly all citizens of civilized countries now enjoy the use of good roads, germ-free water, police protection, free libraries and probably free education of a kind. Public education in England has been meanly starved of money, but it has nevertheless improved, largely owing to the devoted efforts of the teachers, and the habit of reading has become enormously more widespread.

To an increasing extent the rich and the poor read the same books, and they also see the same films and listen to the same radio programmes. And the differences in their way of life have been diminished by the mass-production of cheap clothes and improvements in housing. So far as outward appearance goes, the clothes of rich and poor, especially in the case of women, differ far less than they did thirty or even fifteen years ago. As to housing, England still has slums which are a blot on civilization, but much building has been done during the past ten years, largely by the local authorities. The modern council house, with its bathroom and electric light, is smaller than the stockbroker's villa, but it is recognizably the same kind of house, which the farm labourer's cottage is not. A person who has grown up in a council housing estate is likely to be—indeed, visibly is— more middle class in outlook than a person who has grown up in a slum.

The effect of all this is a general softening of manners. It is enhanced by the fact that modern industrial methods tend always to demand less muscular effort and therefore to leave people with more energy when their day's work is done. Many workers in the light industries are less truly manual labourers than is a doctor or a grocer. In tastes, habits, manners and outlook the working class and the middle class are drawing together. The unjust distinctions remain, but the real differences diminish. The old-style 'proletarian'—collarless, unshaven and with muscles warped by heavy labour—still exists, but he is constantly decreasing in numbers; he only predominates in the heavy-industry areas of the north of England.

After 1918 there began to appear something that had never existed in England before: people of indeterminate social class. In 1910 every human being in these islands could be 'placed' in an instant by his clothes, manners and accent. That is no longer the case. Above all, it is not the case in the new townships that have developed as a result of cheap motor cars and the southward shift of industry. The place to look for the germs of the future England is in light-industry areas and along the arterial roads. In Slough, Dagenham, Barnet, Letchworth, Hayes— everywhere, indeed, on the outskirts of great towns—the old pattern is gradually changing into something new. In those vast new wildernesses of glass and brick the sharp distinctions of the older kind of town, with its slums and mansions, or of the country, with its manor-houses and squalid cottages, no longer exist. There are wide gradations of income, but it is the same kind of life that is being lived at different levels, in labour-saving flats or council houses, along the concrete roads and in the naked democracy of the swimming-pools. It is a rather restless, cultureless life, centring round tinned food, *Picture Post*, the radio and the internal combustion engine. It is a civilization in which children grow up with an intimate knowledge of magnetoes and in complete ignorance of the Bible. To that civilization belong the people who are most at home in and most definitely *of* the modern world, the technicians and the higher-paid skilled workers, the airmen and their mechanics, the radio experts, film producers, popular journalists and industrial chemists. They are the indeterminate stratum at which the older class distinctions are beginning to break down.

This war, unless we are defeated, will wipe out most of the existing class privileges. There are every day fewer people who wish them to continue. Nor need we fear that as the pattern changes life in England will lose its peculiar flavour. The new red cities of Greater London are crude enough, but these things are only the rash that accompanies a change. In whatever shape England emerges from the war it will be deeply tinged with the characteristics that I have spoken of earlier. The intellectuals who hope to see it Russianized or Germanized will be disappointed. The gentleness, the hypocrisy, the thoughtlessness, the reverence for law and the hatred of uniforms will remain, along with the suet puddings and the misty skies. It needs some very great disaster, such as prolonged subjugation by a foreign enemy, to destroy a national culture. The Stock Exchange will be pulled down, the horse plough will give way to the tractor, the country houses will be turned into children's holiday camps, the Eton and Harrow match will be forgotten, but England will still be England, an everlasting animal stretching into the future and the past, and, like all living things, having the power to change out of recognition and yet remain the same.

PART II

SHOPKEEPERS AT WAR

I

I began this book to the tune of German bombs, and I begin this second chapter in the added racket of the barrage. The yellow gun flashes are lighting the sky, the splinters are rattling on the housetops, and London Bridge is falling down, falling down, falling down. Anyone able to read a map knows that we are in deadly danger. I do not mean that we are beaten or need be beaten. Almost certainly the outcome depends on our own will. But at this moment we are in the soup, full fathom five, and we have been brought there by follies which we are still committing and which will drown us altogether if we do not mend our ways quickly.

What this war has demonstrated is that private capitalism, that is, an economic system in which land, factories, mines and transport are owned privately and operated solely for profit—*does not work*. It cannot deliver the goods. This fact had been known to millions of people for years past, but nothing ever came of it, because there was no real urge from below to alter the system, and those at the top had trained themselves to be impenetrably stupid on just this point. Argument and propaganda got one nowhere. The lords of property simply sat on their bottoms and proclaimed that all was for the best. Hitler's conquest of Europe, however, was a *physical* debunking of capitalism. War, for all its evil, is at any rate an unanswerable test of strength, like a try-your-grip machine. Great strength returns the penny, and there is no way of faking the result.

When the nautical screw was first invented, there was a controversy that lasted for years as to whether screw-steamers or paddle-steamers were better. The paddle-steamers, like all obsolete things, had their champions, who supported them by ingenious arguments. Finally, however, a distinguished admiral tied a screw-steamer and a paddle steamer of equal horse-power stern to stern and set their engines running. That settled the question once and for all. And it was something similar that happened on the fields of Norway and of Flanders. Once and for all it was proved that a planned economy is stronger than a planless one. But it is necessary here to give some kind of definition to those much-abused words, Socialism and Fascism.

Socialism is usually defined as "common ownership of the means of production". Crudely: the State, representing the whole nation, owns everything, and everyone is a State employee. This does *not* mean that people are stripped of private possessions such as clothes and furniture, but it *does* mean that all productive goods, such as land, mines, ships and machinery, are the property of the State. The State is the sole large-scale producer. It is not certain that Socialism is in all ways superior to capitalism, but it is certain that, unlike capitalism, it can solve the problems of production and consumption. At normal times a capitalist economy can never consume all that it produces, so that there is always a wasted surplus (wheat burned in furnaces, herrings dumped back into the sea etc etc) and always unemployment. In time of war, on the other hand, it has difficulty in producing all that it needs, because nothing is produced unless someone sees his way to making a profit out of it. In a Socialist economy these problems do not exist. The State simply calculates what goods will be needed and does its best to produce them. Production is only limited by the amount of labour and raw materials. Money, for internal purposes, ceases to be a mysterious all-powerful thing and becomes a sort of coupon or ration-ticket, issued in sufficient quantities to buy up such consumption goods as may be available at the moment.

However, it has become clear in the last few years that "common ownership of the means of production" is not in itself a sufficient definition of Socialism. One must also add the following: approximate equality of incomes (it need be no more than approximate), political democracy, and abolition of all hereditary privilege, especially in education. These are simply the necessary safeguards against the reappearance of a class system. Centralised ownership has very little meaning unless the mass of the people are living roughly upon an equal level, and have some kind of control over the government. "The State" may come to mean no more than a self-elected political party, and oligarchy and privilege can return, based on power rather than on money.

But what then is Fascism?

Fascism, at any rate the German version, is a form of capitalism that borrows from Socialism just such features as will make it efficient for war purposes. Internally, Germany has a good deal in common with a Socialist state. Ownership has never been abolished, there are still capitalists and workers, and—this is the important point, and the real reason why rich men all over the world tend to sympathise with Fascism— generally speaking the same people are capitalists and the same people workers as before the Nazi revolution. But at the same time the State, which is simply the Nazi Party, is in control of everything. It controls investment, raw materials, rates of interest, working hours, wages. The factory owner still owns his factory, but he is for practical purposes reduced to the status of a manager. Everyone is in effect a State employee, though the salaries vary very greatly. The mere *efficiency* of such a system, the elimination of waste and obstruction, is obvious. In seven years it has built up the most powerful war machine the world has ever seen.

But the idea underlying Fascism is irreconcilably different from that which underlies Socialism. Socialism aims, ultimately, at a world-state of free and equal human beings. It takes the equality of human rights for granted. Nazism assumes just the opposite. The driving force behind the Nazi movement is the belief in human *inequality*, the superiority of Germans to all other races, the right of Germany to rule the world. Outside the German Reich it does not recognise any obligations. Eminent Nazi professors have "proved" over and over again that only Nordic man is fully human, have even mooted the idea that non Nordic peoples (such as ourselves) can interbreed with gorillas! Therefore, while a species of war-Socialism exists within the German state, its attitude towards conquered nations is frankly that of an exploiter. The function of the Czechs, Poles, French, etc is simply to produce such goods as Germany may need, and get in return just as little as will keep them from open rebellion. If we are conquered, our job will probably be to manufacture weapons for Hitler's forthcoming wars with Russia and America. The Nazis aim, in effect, at setting up a kind of caste system, with four main castes corresponding rather closely to those of the Hindu religion. At the top comes the Nazi party, second come the mass of the German people, third come the conquered European populations. Fourth and last are to come the coloured peoples, the "semi-apes" as Hitler calls them, who are to be reduced quite openly to slavery.

However horrible this system may seem to us, *it works*. It works because it is a planned system geared to a definite purpose, world conquest, and not allowing any private interest, either of capitalist or worker, to stand in its way. British capitalism does not work, because it is a competitive system in which private profit is and must be the main objective. It is a system in which all the forces are pulling in opposite directions and the interests of the individual are as often as not totally opposed to those of the State.

All through the critical years British capitalism, with its

immense industrial plant and its unrivalled supply of skilled labour, was unequal to the strain of preparing for war. To prepare for war on the modern scale you have got to divert the greater part of your national income to armaments, which means cutting down on consumption goods. A bombing plane, for instance, is equivalent in price to fifty small motor cars, or eighty thousand pairs of silk stockings, or a million loaves of bread. Clearly you can't have *many* bombing planes without lowering the national standard of life. It is guns or butter, as Marshal Goering remarked. But in Chamberlain's England the transition could not be made. The rich would not face the necessary taxation, and while the rich are still visibly rich it is not possible to tax the poor very heavily either. Moreover, so long as *profit* was the main object the manufacturer had no incentive to change over from consumption goods to armaments. A businessman's first duty is to his shareholders. Perhaps England needs tanks, but perhaps it pays better to manufacture motor cars. To prevent war material from reaching the enemy is common sense, but to sell in the highest market is a business duty. Right at the end of August 1939 the British dealers were tumbling over one another in their eagerness to sell Germany tin, rubber, copper and shellac-and this in the clear, certain knowledge that war was going to break out in a week or two. It was about as sensible as selling somebody a razor to cut your throat with. But it was "good business".

And now look at the results. After 1934 it was known that Germany was rearming. After 1936 everyone with eyes in his head knew that war was coming. After Munich it was merely a question of how soon the war would begin. In September 1939 war broke out. *Eight months later* it was discovered that, so far as equipment went, the British army was barely beyond the standard of 1918. We saw our soldiers fighting their way desperately to the coast, with one aeroplane against three, with rifles against tanks, with bayonets against tommy-guns. There were not even enough revolvers to supply all the officers. After a year of war the regular army was still short of 300,000 tin hats. There had even, previously, been a shortage of uniforms—this in one of the greatest woollen-goods producing countries in the world!

What had happened was that the whole moneyed class, unwilling to face a change in their way of life, had shut their eyes to the nature of Fascism and modern war. And false optimism was fed to the general public by the gutter press, which lives on its advertisements and is therefore interested in keeping trade conditions normal. Year after year the Beaverbrook press assured us in huge headlines that *there will be no war,* and as late as the beginning of 1939 Lord Rothermere was describing Hitler as "a great gentleman". And while England in the moment of disaster proved to be short of every war material except ships, it is not recorded that there was any shortage of motor cars, fur coats, gramophones, lipstick, chocolates or silk stockings. And dare anyone pretend that the same tug-of-war between private profit and public necessity is not still continuing? England fights for her life, but business must fight for profits. You can hardly open a newspaper without seeing the two contradictory processes happening side by side. On the very same page you will find the Government urging you to save and the seller of some useless luxury urging you to spend. Lend to Defend, but Guinness is Good for You. Buy a Spitfire, but also buy Haig and Haig, Pond's Face Cream and Black Magic Chocolates.

But one thing gives hope—the visible swing in public opinion. If we can survive this war, the defeat in Flanders will turn out to have been one of the great turning-points in English history. In that spectacular disaster the working class, the middle class and even a section of the business community could see the utter rottenness of private capitalism. Before that the case against capitalism had never been *proved.* Russia, the only definitely Socialist country, was backward and far away. All criticism broke itself against the rat-trap faces of bankers and the brassy laughter of stockbrokers. Socialism? Ha! ha! ha! Where's the money to come from? Ha! ha! ha! The lords of property were firm in their seats, and they knew it. But after the French collapse there came something that could not be laughed away, something that neither chequebooks nor policemen were any use against the bombing. Zweee—*boom*! What's that? Oh, only a bomb on the Stock Exchange. Zweee—*boom*! Another acre of somebody's valuable slum-property gone west. Hitler will at any rate go down in history as the man who made the City of London laugh on the wrong side of its face. For the first time in their lives the comfortable were uncomfortable, the professional optimists had to admit that there was something wrong. It was a great step forward. From that time onwards the ghastly job of trying to convince artificially stupefied people that a planned economy might be better than a free-for-all in which the worst man wins-that job will never be quite so ghastly again.

II

The difference between Socialism and capitalism is not primarily a difference of technique. One cannot simply change from one system to the other as one might install a new piece of machinery in a factory, and then carry on as before, with the same people in positions of control. Obviously there is also needed a complete shift of power. New blood, new men, new ideas—in the true sense of the word, a revolution.

I have spoken earlier of the soundness and homogeneity of England, the patriotism that runs like a connecting thread through almost all classes. After Dunkirk anyone who had eyes in his head could see this. But it is absurd to pretend that the promise of that moment has been fulfilled. Almost certainly the mass of the people are now ready for the vast changes that are necessary; but those changes have not even begun to happen.

England is a family with the wrong members in control. Almost entirely we are governed by the rich, and by people who step into positions of command by right of birth. Few if any of these people are consciously treacherous, some of them are not even fools, but as a class they are quite incapable of leading us to victory. They could not do it, even if their material interests did not constantly trip them up. As I pointed out earlier, they have been artificially stupefied. Quite apart from anything else, the rule of money sees to it that we shall be governed largely by the old—that is, by people utterly unable to grasp what age they are living in or what enemy they are fighting. Nothing was more desolating at the beginning of this war than the way in which the whole of the older generation conspired to pretend that it was the war of 1914-18 over again. All the old duds were back on the job, twenty years older, with the skull plainer in their faces. Ian Hay was cheering up the troops, Belloc was writing articles on strategy, Maurois doing broadcasts, Bairnsfather drawing cartoons. It was like a tea-party of ghosts. And that state of affairs has barely altered. The shock of disaster brought a few able men like Bevin to the front, but in general we are still commanded by people who managed to live through the years 1931-9 without even discovering that Hitler was dangerous. A generation of the unteachable is hanging upon us like a necklace of corpses.

As soon as one considers any problem of this war—and it does not matter whether it is the widest aspect of strategy or the tiniest detail of home organisation—one sees that the necessary moves cannot be made while the social structure of England remains what it is. Inevitably, because of their position and upbringing, the ruling class are fighting for their own privileges, which cannot possibly be reconciled with the public interest. It is a mistake to imagine that war aims, strategy, propaganda and industrial organisation exist in watertight compartments. All are interconnected. Every strategic plan, every tactical method, even every weapon will bear the stamp of the social system that produced it. The British ruling class are fighting against Hitler, whom they have always regarded and whom some of them still regard as their protector against Bolshevism. That does not mean that they will deliberately sell out; but it does mean that at every decisive moment they are likely to falter, pull their punches, do the wrong thing.

Until the Churchill Government called some sort of halt to the process, they have done the wrong thing with an unerring instinct ever since 1931. They helped Franco to overthrow the Spanish Government, although anyone not an imbecile could have told them that a Fascist Spain would be hostile to England. They fed Italy with war materials all through the winter of 1939-40, although it was obvious to the whole world that the Italians were going to attack us in the spring. For the sake of a few hundred thousand dividend drawers they are turning India from an ally into an enemy. Moreover, so long as the moneyed classes remain in control, we cannot develop any but a *defensive* strategy. Every victory means a change in the *status quo*. How can we drive the Italians out of Abyssinia without rousing echoes among the coloured peoples of our own Empire? How can we even smash Hitler without the risk of bringing the German Socialists and Communists into power? The left-wingers who wail that "this is a capitalist war" and that "British Imperialism" is fighting for loot have got their heads screwed on backwards. The last thing the British moneyed class wish for is to acquire fresh territory. It would simply be an embarrassment. Their war aim (both unattainable and unmentionable) is simply to hang on to what they have got.

Internally, England is still the rich man's Paradise. All talk of "equality of sacrifice" is nonsense. At the same time as factory workers are asked to put up with longer hours, advertisements for "Butler. One in family, eight in staff" are appearing in the press. The bombed-out populations of the East End go hungry and homeless while wealthier victims simply step into their cars and flee to comfortable country houses. The Home Guard swells to a million men in a few weeks, and is deliberately organised from above in such a way that only people with private incomes can hold positions of command. Even the rationing system is so arranged that it hits the poor all the time, while people with over £2,000 a year are practically unaffected by it. Everywhere privilege is squandering good will. In such circumstances even propaganda becomes almost impossible. As attempts to stir up patriotic feeling, the red posters issued by the Chamberlain Government at the beginning of the war broke all depth-records. Yet they could not have been much other than they were, for how could Chamberlain and his followers take the risk of rousing strong popular feeling *against fascism*? Anyone who was genuinely hostile to Fascism must also be opposed to Chamberlain himself and to all the others who had helped Hitler into power. So also with external propaganda. In all Lord Halifax's speeches there is not one concrete proposal for which a single inhabitant of Europe would risk the top joint of his little finger. For what war-aim can Halifax, or anyone like him, conceivably have, except to put the clock back to 1933?

It is only by revolution that the native genius of the English people can be set free. Revolution does not mean red flags and street fighting, it means a fundamental shift of power. Whether it happens with or without bloodshed is largely an accident of time and place. Nor does it mean the dictatorship of a single class. The people in England who grasp what changes are needed and are capable of carrying them through are not confined to any one class, though it is true that very few people with over £2,000 a year are among them. What is wanted is a conscious open revolt by ordinary people against inefficiency, class privilege and the rule of the old. It is not primarily a question of change of government. British governments do, broadly speaking, represent the will of the people, and if we alter our structure from below we shall get the government we need. Ambassadors, generals, officials and colonial administrators who are senile or pro-Fascist are more dangerous than Cabinet ministers whose follies have to be committed in public. Right through our national life we have got to fight against privilege, against the notion that a half-witted public-schoolboy is better fitted for command than an intelligent mechanic. Although there are gifted and honest *individuals* among them, we have got to break the grip of the moneyed class as a whole. England has got to assume its real shape. The England that is only just beneath the surface, in the factories and the newspaper offices, in the aeroplanes and the submarines, has got to take charge of its own destiny.

In the short run, equality of sacrifice, "war-Communism", is even more important than radical economic changes. It is very necessary that industry should be nationalised, but it is more urgently necessary that such monstrosities as butlers and "private incomes" should disappear forthwith. Almost certainly the main reason why the Spanish Republic could keep up the fight for two and a half years against impossible odds was that there were no gross contrasts of wealth. The people suffered horribly, but they all suffered alike. When the private soldier had not a cigarette, the general had not one either. Given equality of sacrifice, the morale of a country like England would probably be unbreakable. But at present we have nothing to appeal to except traditional patriotism, which is deeper here than elsewhere, but is not necessarily bottomless. At some point or another you have got to deal with the man who says "I should be no worse off under Hitler". But what answer can you give him—that is, what answer that you can expect him to listen to—while common soldiers risk their lives for two and sixpence a day, and fat women ride about in Rolls-Royce cars, nursing pekineses?

It is quite likely that this war will last three years. It will mean cruel overwork, cold dull winters, uninteresting food, lack of amusements, prolonged bombing. It cannot but lower the general standard of living, because the essential act of war is to manufacture armaments instead of consumable goods. The working class will have to suffer terrible things. And they *will* suffer them, almost indefinitely, provided that they know what they are fighting for. They are not cowards, and they are not even internationally minded. They can stand all that the

Spanish workers stood, and more. But they will want some kind of proof that a better life is ahead for themselves and their children. The one sure earnest of that is that when they are taxed and overworked they shall see that the rich are being hit even harder. And if the rich squeal audibly, so much the better.

We can bring these things about, if we really want to. It is not true that public opinion has no power in England. It never makes itself heard without achieving something; it has been responsible for most of the changes for the better during the past six months. But we have moved with glacier-like slowness, and we have learned only from disasters. It took the fall of Paris to get rid of Chamberlain and the unnecessary suffering of scores of thousands of people in the East End to get rid or partially rid of Sir John Anderson. It is not worth losing a battle in order to bury a corpse. For we are fighting against swift evil intelligences, and time presses, and:

history to the defeated May say Alas! but cannot alter or pardon.

III

During the last six months there has been much talk of "the Fifth Column". From time to time obscure lunatics have been jailed for making speeches in favour of Hitler, and large numbers of German refugees have been interned, a thing which has almost certainly done us great harm in Europe. It is of course obvious that the idea of a large, organised army of Fifth Columnists suddenly appearing on the streets with weapons in their hands, as in Holland and Belgium, is ridiculous. Nevertheless a Fifth Column danger does exist. One can only consider it if one also considers in what way England might be defeated.

It does not seem probable that air bombing can settle a major war. England might well be invaded and conquered, but the invasion would be a dangerous gamble, and if it happened and failed it would probably leave us more united and less Blimp-ridden than before. Moreover, if England were overrun by foreign troops the English people would know that they had been beaten and would continue the struggle. It is doubtful whether they could be held down permanently, or whether Hitler wishes to keep an army of a million men stationed in these islands. A government of ——,—— and —— (you can fill in the names) would suit him better. The English can probably not be bullied into surrender, but they might quite easily be bored, cajoled or cheated into it, provided that, as at Munich, they did not know that they were surrendering. It could happen most easily when the war seemed to be going well rather than badly. The threatening tone of so much of the German and Italian propaganda is a psychological mistake. It only gets home on intellectuals. With the general public the proper approach would be "Let's call it a draw". It is when a peace-offer along *those* lines is made that the pro-Fascists will raise their voices.

But who are the pro-Fascists? The idea of a Hitler victory appeals to the very rich, to the Communists, to Mosley's followers, to the pacifists, and to certain sections among the Catholics. Also, if things went badly enough on the Home Front, the whole of the poorer section of the working class might swing round to a position that was defeatist though not actively pro-Hitler.

In this motley list one can see the daring of German propaganda, its willingness to offer everything to everybody. But the various pro-Fascist forces are not consciously acting together, and they operate in different ways.

The Communists must certainly be regarded as pro-Hitler, and are bound to remain so unless Russian policy changes, but they have not very much influence. Mosley's Blackshirts, though now lying very low, are a more serious danger, because of the footing they probably possess in the armed forces. Still, even in its palmiest days Mosley's following can hardly have numbered 50,000. Pacifism is a psychological curiosity rather than a political movement. Some of the extremer pacifists, starting out with a complete renunciation of violence, have ended by warmly championing Hitler and even toying with Antisemitism. This is interesting, but it is not important. "Pure" pacifism, which is a by-product of naval power, can only appeal to people in very sheltered positions. Moreover, being negative and irresponsible, it does not inspire much devotion. Of the membership of the Peace Pledge Union, less than 15 per cent even pay their annual subscriptions. None of these bodies of people, pacifists, Communists or Blackshirts, could bring a large scale stop-the-war movement into being by their own efforts. But they might help to make things very much easier for a treacherous government negotiating surrender. Like the French Communists, they might become the half-conscious agents of millionaires.

The real danger is from above. One ought not to pay any attention to Hitler's recent line of talk about being the friend of the poor man, the enemy of plutocracy, etc etc. Hitler's real self is in *Mein Kampf*, and in his actions. He has never persecuted the rich, except when they were Jews or when they tried actively to oppose him. He stands for a centralised economy which robs the capitalist of most of his power but leaves the structure of society much as before. The State controls industry, but there are still rich and poor, masters and men. Therefore, as against genuine Socialism, the moneyed class have always been on his side. This was crystal clear at the time of the Spanish civil war, and clear again at the time when France surrendered. Hitler's puppet government are not working men, but a gang of bankers, gaga generals and corrupt right wing politicians.

That kind of spectacular, *conscious* treachery is less likely to succeed in England, indeed is far less likely even to be tried. Nevertheless, to many payers of supertax this war is simply an insane family squabble which ought to be stopped at all costs. One need not doubt that a "peace" movement is on foot somewhere in high places; probably a shadow Cabinet has already been formed. These people will get their chance not in the moment of defeat but in some stagnant period when boredom is reinforced by discontent. They will not talk about surrender, only about peace; and doubtless they will persuade themselves, and perhaps other people, that they are acting for the best. An army of unemployed led by millionaires quoting the Sermon on the Mount—that is our danger. But it cannot arise when we have once introduced a reasonable degree of social justice. The lady in the Rolls-Royce car is more damaging to morale than a fleet of Goering's bombing planes.

PART III

THE ENGLISH REVOLUTION

I

The English revolution started several years ago, and it began to gather momentum when the troops came back from Dunkirk. Like all else in England, it happens in a sleepy, unwilling way, but it is happening. The war has speeded it up, but it has also increased, and desperately, the necessity for speed.

Progress and reaction are ceasing to have anything to do with party labels. If one wishes to name a particular moment, one can say that the old distinction between Right and Left broke down when *Picture Post* was first published. What are the politics of *Picture Post*? Or of *Cavalcade*, or Priestley's broadcasts, or the leading articles in the *Evening Standard*? None of the old classifications will fit them. They merely point to the existence of multitudes of unlabelled people who have grasped within the last year or two that something is wrong. But since a classless, ownerless society is generally spoken of as "Socialism", we can give that name to the society towards which we are now moving. The war and the revolution are inseparable. We cannot establish anything that a western nation would regard as Socialism without defeating Hitler; on the other hand we cannot defeat Hitler while we remain economically and socially in the nineteenth century.

The past is fighting the future and we have two years, a year, possibly only a few months, to see to it that the future wins.

We cannot look to this or to any similar government to put through the necessary changes of its own accord. The initiative will have to come from below. That means that there will have to arise something that has never existed in England, a Socialist movement that actually has the mass of the people behind it. But one must start by recognising why it is that English Socialism has failed.

In England there is only one Socialist party that has ever seriously mattered, the Labour Party. It has never been able to achieve any major change, because except in purely domestic matters it has never possessed a genuinely independent policy. It was and is primarily a party of the trade unions, devoted to raising wages and improving working conditions. This meant that all through the critical years it was directly interested in the prosperity of British capitalism. In particular it was interested in the maintenance of the British Empire, for the wealth of England was drawn largely from Asia and Africa. The standard of living of the trade union workers, whom the Labour Party represented, depended indirectly on the sweating of Indian coolies. At the same time the Labour Party was a Socialist party, using Socialist phraseology, thinking in terms of an old-fashioned anti-imperialism and more or less pledged to make restitution to the coloured races. It had to stand for the "independence" of India, just as it had to stand for disarmament and "progress" generally. Nevertheless everyone was aware that this was nonsense. In the age of the tank and the bombing plane, backward agricultural countries like India and the African colonies can no more be independent than can a cat or a dog. Had any Labour government come into office with a clear majority and then proceeded to grant India anything that could truly be called independence, India would simply have been absorbed by Japan, or divided between Japan and Russia.

To a Labour government in power, three imperial policies would have been open. One was to continue administering the

76

Empire exactly as before, which meant dropping all pretensions to Socialism. Another was to set the subject peoples "free", which meant in practice handing them over to Japan, Italy and other predatory powers, and incidentally causing a catastrophic drop in the British standard of living. The third was to develop a *positive* imperial policy, and aim at transforming the Empire into a federation of Socialist states, like a looser and freer version of the Union of Soviet Republics. But the Labour Party's history and background made this impossible. It was a party of the trade unions, hopelessly parochial in outlook, with little interest in imperial affairs and no contacts among the men who actually held the Empire together. It would have had to hand the administration of India and Africa and the whole job of imperial defence to men drawn from a different class and traditionally hostile to Socialism. Overshadowing everything was the doubt whether a Labour government which meant business could make itself obeyed. For all the size of its following, the Labour Party had no footing in the navy, little or none in the army or air force, none whatever in the Colonial Services, and not even a sure footing in the Home Civil Service. In England its position was strong but not unchallengeable, and outside England all the key points were in the hands of its enemies. Once in power, the same dilemma would always have faced it: carry out your promises, and risk revolt, or continue with the same policy as the Conservatives, and stop talking about Socialism. The Labour leaders never found a solution, and from 1935 onwards it was very doubtful whether they had any wish to take office. They had degenerated into a Permanent Opposition.

Outside the Labour Party there existed several extremist parties, of whom the Communists were the strongest. The Communists had considerable influence in the Labour Party in the years 1920-6 and 1935-9. Their chief importance, and that of the whole left wing of the Labour movement, was the part they played in alienating the middle classes from Socialism.

The history of the past seven years has made it perfectly clear that Communism has no chance in western Europe. The appeal of Fascism is enormously greater. In one country after another the Communists have been rooted out by their more up-to-date enemies, the Nazis. In the English-speaking countries they never had a serious footing. The creed they were spreading could appeal only to a rather rare type of person, found chiefly in the middle-class intelligentsia, the type who has ceased to love his own country but still feels the need of patriotism, and therefore develops patriotic sentiments towards Russia. By 1940, after working for twenty years and spending a great deal of money, the British Communists had barely 20,000 members, actually a smaller number than they had started out with in 1920. The other Marxist parties were of even less importance. They had not the Russian money and prestige behind them, and even more than the Communists they were tied to the nineteenth-century doctrine of the class war. They continued year after year to preach this out-of-date gospel, and never drew any inference from the fact that it got them no followers.

Nor did any strong native Fascist movement grow up. Material conditions were not bad enough, and no leader who could be taken seriously was forthcoming. One would have had to look a long time to find a man more barren of ideas than Sir Oswald Mosley. He was as hollow as a jug. Even the elementary fact that Fascism must not offend national sentiment had escaped him. His entire movement was imitated slavishly from abroad, the uniform and the party programme from Italy and the salute from Germany, with the Jew baiting tacked on as an afterthought, Mosley having actually started his movement with Jews among his most prominent followers. A man of the stamp of Bottomley or Lloyd George could perhaps have brought a real British Fascist movement into existence. But such leaders only appear when the psychological need for them exists.

After twenty years of stagnation and unemployment, the entire English Socialist movement was unable to produce a version of Socialism which the mass of the people could even find desirable. The Labour Party stood for a timid reformism, the Marxists were looking at the modern world through nineteenth-century spectacles. Both ignored agriculture and imperial problems, and both antagonised the middle classes. The suffocating stupidity of left-wing propaganda had frightened away whole classes of necessary people, factory managers, airmen, naval officers, farmers, white-collar workers, shopkeepers, policemen. All of these people had been taught to think of Socialism as something which menaced their livelihood, or as something seditious, alien, "anti-British" as they would have called it. Only the intellectuals, the least useful section of the middle class, gravitated towards the movement.

A Socialist Party which genuinely wished to achieve anything would have started by facing several facts which to this day are considered unmentionable in left-wing circles. It would have recognised that England is more united than most countries, that the British workers have a great deal to lose besides their chains, and that the differences in outlook and habits between class and class are rapidly diminishing. In general, it would have recognised that the old-fashioned "proletarian revolution" is an impossibility. But all through the between-war years no Socialist programme that was both revolutionary and workable ever appeared; basically, no doubt, because no one genuinely wanted any major change to happen. The Labour leaders wanted to go on and on, drawing their salaries and periodically swapping jobs with the Conservatives. The Communists wanted to go on and on, suffering a comfortable martyrdom, meeting with endless defeats and afterwards putting the blame on other people. The left-wing intelligentsia wanted to go on and on, sniggering at the Blimps, sapping away at middle-class morale, but still keeping their favoured position as hangers-on of the dividend-drawers. Labour Party politics had become a variant of Conservatism, "revolutionary" politics had become a game of make-believe.

Now, however, the circumstances have changed, the drowsy

years have ended. Being a Socialist no longer means kicking theoretically against a system which in practice you are fairly well satisfied with. This time our predicament is real. It is "the Philistines be upon thee, Samson". We have got to make our words take physical shape, or perish. We know very well that with its present social structure England cannot survive, and we have got to make other people see that fact and act upon it. We cannot win the war without introducing Socialism, nor establish Socialism without winning the war. At such a time it is possible, as it was not in the peaceful years, to be both revolutionary and realistic. A Socialist movement which can swing the mass of the people behind it, drive the pro-Fascists out of positions of control, wipe out the grosser injustices and let the working class see that they have something to fight for, win over the middle classes instead of antagonising them, produce a workable imperial policy instead of a mixture of humbug and Utopianism, bring patriotism and intelligence into partnership—for the first time, a movement of such a kind becomes possible.

II

The fact that we are at war has turned Socialism from a textbook word into a realisable policy.

The inefficiency of private capitalism has been proved all over Europe. Its injustice has been proved in the East End of London. Patriotism, against which the Socialists fought so long, has become a tremendous lever in their hands. People who at any other time would cling like glue to their miserable scraps of privilege, will surrender them fast enough when their country is in danger. War is the greatest of all agents of change. It speeds up all processes, wipes out minor distinctions, brings realities to the surface. Above all, war brings it home to the individual that he is not altogether an individual. It is only because they are aware of this that men will die on the field of battle. At this moment it is not so much a question of surrendering life as of surrendering leisure, comfort, economic liberty, social prestige. There are very few people in England who really want to see their country conquered by Germany. If it can be made clear that defeating Hitler means wiping out class privilege, the great mass of middling people, the £6 a week to £2,000 a year class, will probably be on our side. These people are quite indispensable, because they include most of the technical experts. Obviously the snobbishness and political ignorance of people like airmen and naval officers will be a very great difficulty. But without those airmen, destroyer commanders, etc etc we could not survive for a week. The only approach to them is through their patriotism. An intelligent Socialist movement will use their patriotism, instead of merely insulting it, as hitherto.

But do I mean that there will be no opposition? Of course not. It would be childish to expect anything of the kind.

There will be a bitter political struggle, and there will be unconscious and half-conscious sabotage everywhere. At some point or other it may be necessary to use violence. It is easy to imagine a pro-Fascist rebellion breaking out in, for instance, India. We shall have to fight against bribery, ignorance and snobbery. The bankers and the larger businessmen, the landowners and dividend-drawers, the officials with their prehensile bottoms, will obstruct for all they are worth. Even the middle classes will writhe when their accustomed way of life is menaced. But just because the English sense of national unity has never disintegrated, because patriotism is finally stronger than class hatred, the chances are that the will of the majority will prevail. It is no use imagining that one can make fundamental changes without causing a split in the nation; but the treacherous minority will be far smaller in time of war than it would be at any other time.

The swing of opinion is visibly happening, but it cannot be counted on to happen fast enough of its own accord. This war is a race between the consolidation of Hitler's empire and the growth of democratic consciousness. Everywhere in England you can see a ding-dong battle ranging to and fro—in Parliament and in the Government, in the factories and the armed forces, in the pubs and the air-raid shelters, in the newspapers and on the radio. Every day there are tiny defeats, tiny victories. Morrison for Home Security—a few yards forward. Priestley shoved off the air—a few yards back. It is a struggle between the groping and the unteachable, between the young and the old, between the living and the dead. But it is very necessary that the discontent which undoubtedly exists should take a purposeful and not merely obstructive form. It is time for *the people* to define their war-aims. What is wanted is a simple, concrete programme of action, which can be given all possible publicity, and round which public opinion can group itself.

I suggest that the following six-point programme is the kind of thing we need. The first three points deal with England's internal policy, the other three with the Empire and the world:

1. Nationalisation of land, mines, railways,
   banks and major industries.
2. Limitation of incomes, on such a scale that
   the highest tax free income in Britain does not
   exceed the lowest by more than ten to one.
3. Reform of the educational system along democratic lines.
4. Immediate Dominion status for India, with
   power to secede when the war is over.
5. Formation of an Imperial General Council, in which
   the coloured peoples are to be represented.
6. Declaration of formal alliance with China, Abyssinia
   and all other victims of the Fascist powers.

The general tendency of this programme is unmistakable. It aims quite frankly at turning this war into a revolutionary war and England into a Socialist democracy. I have deliberately included in it nothing that the simplest person could not understand and see the reason for. In the form in which I have put it, it could be printed on the front page of the *Daily Mirror*. But for the purposes of this book a certain amount of amplification is needed.

1. NATIONALISATION

One can "nationalise" industry by the stroke of a pen, but the actual process is slow and complicated. What is needed is that the ownership of all major industry shall be formally vested in the State, representing the common people. Once that is done it becomes possible to eliminate the class of mere *owners* who live not by virtue of anything they produce but by the possession of title-deeds and share certificates. State-ownership implies, therefore, that nobody shall live without working. How sudden a change in the conduct of industry it implies is less certain. In a country like England we cannot rip down the whole structure and build again from the bottom, least of all in time of war. Inevitably the majority of industrial concerns will continue with much the same personnel as before, the one-time owners or managing directors carrying on with their jobs as State employees. There is reason to think that many of the smaller capitalists would actually welcome some such arrangement. The resistance will come from the big capitalists, the bankers, the landlords and the idle rich, roughly speaking the class with over £2,000 a year—and even if one counts in all their dependants there are not more than half a million of these people in England. Nationalisation of agricultural land implies cutting out the landlord and the tithe drawer, but not necessarily interfering with the farmer. It is difficult to imagine any reorganisation of English agriculture that would not retain most of the existing farms as units, at any rate at the beginning. The farmer, when he is competent, will continue as a salaried manager. He is virtually that already, with the added disadvantage of having to make a profit and being permanently in debt to the bank. With certain kinds of petty trading, and even the small-scale ownership of land, the State will probably not interfere at all. It would be a great mistake to start by victimising the smallholder class, for instance. These people are necessary, on the whole they are competent, and the amount of work they do depends on the feeling that they are "their own masters". But the State will certainly impose an upward limit to the ownership of land (probably fifteen acres at the very most), and will never permit any ownership of land in town areas.

From the moment that all productive goods have been declared the property of the State, the common people will feel, as they cannot feel now, that the State is *themselves*. They will be ready then to endure the sacrifices that are ahead of us, war or no war. And even if the face of England hardly seems to change, on the day that our main industries are formally nationalised the dominance of a single class will have been broken. From then onwards the emphasis will be shifted from ownership to management, from privilege to competence. It is quite possible that State-ownership will in itself bring about less social change than will be forced upon us by the common hardships of war. But it is the necessary first step without which any *real* reconstruction is impossible.

2. INCOMES

Limitation of incomes implies the fixing of a minimum wage, which implies a managed internal currency based simply on the amount of consumption goods available. And this again implies a stricter rationing scheme than is now in operation. It is no use at this stage of the world's history to suggest that all human beings should have *exactly* equal incomes. It has been shown over and over again that without some kind of money reward there is no incentive to undertake certain jobs. On the other hand the money reward need not be very large. In practice it is impossible that earnings should be limited quite as rigidly as I have suggested. There will always be anomalies and evasions. But there is no reason why ten to one should not be the maximum normal variation. And within those limits some sense of equality is possible. A man with £3 a week and a man with £1,500 a year can feel themselves fellow creatures, which the Duke of Westminster and the sleepers on the Embankment benches cannot.

3. EDUCATION

In wartime, educational reform must necessarily be promise rather than performance. At the moment we are not in a position to raise the school-leaving age or increase the teaching staffs of the elementary schools. But there are certain immediate steps that we could take towards a democratic educational system. We could start by abolishing the autonomy of the public schools and the older universities and flooding them with State-aided pupils chosen simply on grounds of ability. At present, public-school education is partly a training in class prejudice and partly a sort of tax that the middle classes pay to the upper class in return for the right to enter certain professions. It is true that that state of affairs is altering. The middle classes have begun to rebel against the expensiveness of education, and the war will bankrupt the majority of the public schools if it continues for another year or two. The evacuation is also producing certain minor changes. But there is a danger that some of the older schools, which will be able to weather the financial storm longest, will survive in some form or another as festering centres of snobbery. As for the 10,000 "private" schools that England possesses, the vast majority of them deserve nothing except suppression. They are simply commercial undertakings, and in many cases their educational level is actually lower than that of the elementary schools. They merely exist because of a widespread idea that there is something disgraceful in being educated by the public authorities. The State could quell this idea by declaring itself responsible for all education, even if at the start this were no more than a gesture. We need gestures as well as actions. It is all too obvious that our talk of "defending democracy" is nonsense while it is a mere accident of birth that decides whether a gifted child shall or shall not get the education it deserves.

4. INDIA

What we must offer India is not "freedom", which, as I have said earlier, is impossible, but alliance, partnership-in a word, equality. But we must also tell the Indians that they are free to secede, if they want to. Without that there can be no equality of partnership, and our claim to be defending the coloured peoples against Fascism will never be believed. But it is a mistake to imagine that if the Indians were free to cut themselves adrift they would immediately do so. When a British government *offers* them unconditional independence, they will refuse it. For as soon as they have the power to secede the chief reasons for doing so will have disappeared.

A complete severance of the two countries would be a disaster for India no less than for England. Intelligent Indians know this. As things are at present, India not only cannot defend itself, it is hardly even capable of feeding itself. The whole administration of the country depends on a framework of experts (engineers, forest officers, railwaymen, soldiers, doctors) who are predominantly English and could not be replaced within five or ten years. Moreover, English is the chief lingua franca and nearly the whole of the Indian intelligentsia is deeply Anglicised. Any transference to foreign rule—for if the British marched out of India the Japanese and other powers would immediately march in—would mean an immense dislocation. Neither the Japanese, the Russians, the Germans nor the Italians would be capable of administering India even at the low level of efficiency that is attained by the British. They do not possess the necessary supplies of technical experts or the knowledge of languages and local conditions, and they probably could not win the confidence of indispensable go-betweens such as the Eurasians. If India were simply "liberated", i.e. deprived of British military protection, the first result would be a fresh foreign conquest, and the second a series of enormous famines which would kill millions of people within a few years.

What India needs is the power to work out its own constitution without British interference, but in some kind of partnership that ensures its military protection and technical advice. This is unthinkable until there is a Socialist government in England. For at least eighty years England has artificially prevented the development of India, partly from fear of trade competition if Indian industries were too highly developed, partly because backward peoples are more easily governed than civilised ones. It is a commonplace that the average Indian suffers far more from his own countrymen than from the British. The petty Indian capitalist exploits the town worker with the utmost ruthlessness, the peasant lives from birth to death in the grip of the money-lender. But all this is an indirect result of the British rule, which aims half-consciously at keeping India as backward as possible. The classes most loyal to Britain are the princes, the landowners and the business community—in general, the reactionary classes who are doing fairly well out of the *status quo.*. The moment that England ceased to stand towards India in the relation of an exploiter, the balance of forces would be altered. No need then for the British to flatter the ridiculous Indian princes, with their gilded elephants and cardboard armies, to prevent the growth of the Indian trade unions, to play off Moslem against Hindu, to protect the worthless life of the money-lender, to receive the salaams of toadying minor officials, to prefer the half-barbarous

Gurkha to the educated Bengali. Once check that stream of dividends that flows from the bodies of Indian coolies to the banking accounts of old ladies in Cheltenham, and the whole sahib-native nexus, with its haughty ignorance on one side and envy and servility on the other, can come to an end. Englishmen and Indians can work side by side for the development of India, and for the training of Indians in all the arts which, so far, they have been systematically prevented from learning. How many of the existing British personnel in India, commercial or official, would fall in with such an arrangement—which would mean ceasing once and for all to be "sahibs"—is a different question. But, broadly speaking, more is to be hoped from the younger men and from those officials (civil engineers, forestry and agricultural experts, doctors, educationists) who have been scientifically educated. The higher officials, the provincial governors, commissioners, judges, etc are hopeless; but they are also the most easily replaceable.

That, roughly, is what would be meant by Dominion status if it were offered to India by a Socialist government. It is an offer of partnership on equal terms until such time as the world has ceased to be ruled by bombing planes. But we must add to it the unconditional right to secede. It is the only way of proving that we mean what we say. And what applies to India applies, *mutatis mutandis*, to Burma, Malaya and most of our African possessions.

5 and 6 explain themselves. They are the necessary preliminary to any claim that we are fighting this war for the protection of peaceful peoples against Fascist aggression.

Is it impossibly hopeful to think that such a policy as this could get a following in England? A year ago, even six months ago, it would have been, but not now. Moreover-and this is the peculiar opportunity of this moment—it could be given the necessary publicity. There is now a considerable weekly press, with a circulation of millions, which would be ready to popularise—if not *exactly* the programme I have sketched above, at any rate *some* policy along those lines. There are even three or four daily papers which would be prepared to give it a sympathetic hearing. That is the distance we have travelled in the last six months.

But is such a policy realisable? That depends entirely on ourselves.

Some of the points I have suggested are of the kind that could be carried out immediately, others would take years or decades and even then would not be perfectly achieved. No political programme is ever carried out in its entirety. But what matters is that that or something like it should be our declared policy. It is always the *direction* that counts. It is of course quite hopeless to expect the present Government to pledge itself to any policy that implies turning this war into a revolutionary war. It is at best a government of compromise, with Churchill riding two horses like a circus acrobat. Before such measures as limitation of incomes become even thinkable, there will have to be a complete shift of power away from the old ruling class. If during this winter the war settles into another stagnant period, we ought in my opinion to agitate for a General Election, a thing which the Tory Party machine will make frantic efforts to prevent. But even without an election we can get the government we want, provided that we want it urgently enough. A real shove from below will accomplish it. As to who will be in that government when it comes, I make no guess. I only know that the right men will be there when the people really want them, for it is movements that make leaders and not leaders movements.

Within a year, perhaps even within six months, if we are still unconquered, we shall see the rise of something that has never existed before, a specifically *English* Socialist movement. Hitherto there has been only the Labour Party, which was the creation of the working class but did not aim at any fundamental change, and Marxism, which was a German theory interpreted by Russians and unsuccessfully transplanted to England. There was nothing that really touched the heart of the English people.

Throughout its entire history the English Socialist movement has never produced a song with a catchy tune—nothing like *La Marseillaise* or *La Cucuracha*, for instance. When a Socialist movement native to England appears, the Marxists, like all others with a vested interest in the past, will be its bitter enemies. Inevitably they will denounce it as "Fascism". Already it is customary among the more soft-boiled intellectuals of the Left to declare that if we fight against the Nazis we shall "go Nazi" ourselves. They might almost equally well say that if we fight against Negroes we shall turn black. To "go Nazi" we should have to have the history of Germany behind us. Nations do not escape from their past merely by making a revolution. An English Socialist government will transform the nation from top to bottom, but it will still bear all over it the unmistakable marks of our own civilisation, the peculiar civilisation which I discussed earlier in this book.

It will not be doctrinaire, nor even logical. It will abolish the House of Lords, but quite probably will not abolish the Monarchy. It will leave anachronisms and loose ends everywhere, the judge in his ridiculous horsehair wig and the lion and the unicorn on the soldier's cap-buttons. It will not set up any explicit class dictatorship. It will group itself round the old Labour Party and its mass following will be in the trade unions, but it will draw into it most of the middle class and many of the younger sons of the bourgeoisie. Most of its directing brains will come from the new indeterminate class of skilled workers, technical experts, airmen, scientists, architects and journalists, the people who feel at home in the radio and ferro-concrete age. But it will never lose touch with the tradition of compromise and the belief in a law that is above the State. It will shoot traitors, but it will give them a solemn trial beforehand and occasionally it will acquit them. It will crush any open revolt promptly and cruelly, but it will interfere very little with the spoken and written word. Political parties with different names will still exist, revolutionary sects will still be publishing their newspapers and making as little impression as ever. It will disestablish the Church, but will not persecute religion. It will retain a vague reverence for the Christian moral code, and from time to time will refer to England as "a Christian country". The Catholic Church will war against it, but the Nonconformist sects and the bulk of the Anglican Church will be able to come to terms with it. It will show a power of assimilating the past which will shock foreign observers and sometimes make them doubt whether any revolution has happened.

But all the same it will have done the essential thing. It will have nationalised industry, scaled down incomes, set up a classless educational system. Its real nature will be apparent from the hatred which the surviving rich men of the world will feel for it. It will aim not at disintegrating the Empire but at turning it into a federation of Socialist states, freed not so much from the British flag as from the money-lender, the dividend-drawer and the woodenheaded British official. Its war strategy will be totally different from that of any property-ruled state, because it will not be afraid of the revolutionary after-effects when any existing régime is brought down. It will not have the smallest scruple about attacking hostile neutrals or stirring up native rebellion in enemy colonies. It will fight in such a way that even if it is beaten its memory will be dangerous to the victor, as the memory of the French Revolution was dangerous to Metternich's Europe. The dictators will fear it as they could not fear the existing British régime, even if its military strength were ten times what it is.

But at this moment, when the drowsy life of England has barely altered, and the offensive contrast of wealth and poverty still exists everywhere, even amid the bombs, why do I dare to say that all these things "will" happen?

Because the time has come when one can predict the future in terms of an "either—or". Either we turn this war into a revolutionary war (I do not say that our policy will be *exactly* what I have indicated above—merely that it will be along those

91

general lines) or we lose it, and much more besides. Quite soon it will be possible to say definitely that our feet are set upon one path or the other. But at any rate it is certain that with our present social structure we cannot win. Our real forces, physical, moral or intellectual, cannot be mobilised.

III

Patriotism has nothing to do with Conservatism. It is actually the opposite of Conservatism, since it is a devotion to something that is always changing and yet is felt to be mystically the same. It is the bridge between the future and the past. No real revolutionary has ever been an internationalist.

During the past twenty years the negative, *fainéant* outlook which has been fashionable among English left-wingers, the sniggering of the intellectuals at patriotism and physical courage, the persistent effort to chip away English morale and spread a hedonistic, what-do-I-get-out-of-it attitude to life, has done nothing but harm. It would have been harmful even if we had been living in the squashy League of Nations universe that these people imagined. In an age of Fuehrers and bombing planes it was a disaster. However little we may like it, toughness is the price of survival. A nation trained to think hedonistically cannot survive amid peoples who work like slaves and breed like rabbits, and whose chief national industry is war. English Socialists of nearly all colours have wanted to make a stand against Fascism, but at the same time they have aimed at making their own countrymen unwarlike. They have failed, because in England traditional loyalties are stronger than new ones. But in spite of all the "anti-Fascist" heroics of the left-wing press, what chance should we have stood when the real struggle with Fascism came, if the average Englishman had been the kind of creature that the *New Statesman*, the *Daily Worker* or even the *News Chronicle* wished to make him?

92

Up to 1935 virtually all English left-wingers were vaguely pacifist. After 1935 the more vocal of them flung themselves eagerly into the Popular Front movement, which was simply an evasion of the whole problem posed by Fascism. It set out to be "anti-Fascist" in a purely negative way—"against" Fascism without being "for" any discoverable policy-and underneath it lay the flabby idea that when the time came the Russians would do our fighting for us. It is astonishing how this illusion fails to die. Every week sees its spate of letters to the press, pointing out that if we had a government with no Tories in it the Russians could hardly avoid coming round to our side. Or we are to publish high-sounding war-aims (*vide* books like *Unser Kampf, A Hundred Million Allies, If We Choose,* etc), whereupon the European populations will infallibly rise on our behalf. It is the same idea all the time-look abroad for your inspiration, get someone else to do your fighting for you. Underneath it lies the frightful inferiority complex of the English intellectual, the belief that the English are no longer a martial race, no longer capable of enduring.

In truth there is no reason to think that anyone will do our fighting for us yet awhile, except the Chinese, who have been doing it for three years already. The Russians may be driven to fight on our side by the fact of a direct attack, but they have made it clear enough that they will not stand up to the German army if there is any way of avoiding it. In any case they are not likely to be attracted by the spectacle of a left-wing government in England. The present Russian régime must almost certainly be hostile to any revolution in the West. The subject peoples of Europe will rebel when Hitler begins to totter, but not earlier. Our potential allies are not the Europeans but on the one hand the Americans, who will need a year to mobilise their resources even if Big Business can be brought to heel, and on the other hand the coloured peoples, who cannot be even sentimentally on our side till our own revolution has started. For a long time, a year, two years, possibly three years, England has got to be the shock-absorber of the world. We have got to face bombing, hunger, overwork, influenza, boredom and treacherous peace offers. Manifestly it is a time to stiffen morale, not to weaken it. Instead of taking the mechanically anti-British attitude which is usual on the Left, it is better to consider what the world would really be like if the English-speaking culture perished. For it is childish to suppose that the other English-speaking countries, even the USA, will be unaffected if Britain is conquered.

Lord Halifax, and all his tribe, believe that when the war is over things will be exactly as they were before. Back to the crazy pavement of Versailles, back to "democracy", i.e. capitalism, back to dole queues and the Rolls-Royce cars, back to the grey top hats and the sponge-bag trousers, *in saecula saeculorum*. It is of course obvious that nothing of the kind is going to happen. A feeble imitation of it might just possibly happen in the case of a negotiated peace, but only for a short while. *laissez-faire* capitalism is dead[3]. The choice lies between the kind of collective society that Hitler will set up and the kind that can arise if he is defeated.

If Hitler wins this war he will consolidate his rule over Europe, Africa and the Middle East, and if his armies have not been too greatly exhausted beforehand, he will wrench vast territories from Soviet Russia. He will set up a graded caste-society in which the German *Herrenvolk* ("master race" or "aristocratic race") will rule over Slavs and other lesser peoples whose job it will be to produce low-priced agricultural products. He will reduce the coloured peoples once and for all to outright slavery. The real quarrel of the Fascist powers with British imperialism is that they know that it is disintegrating. Another twenty years along the present line of development,

---

3   It is interesting to notice that Mr Kennedy, USA Ambassador in London, remarked on his return to New York in October 1940 that as a result of the war "democracy is finished". By "democracy", of course, he meant private capitalism.

and India will be a peasant republic linked with England only by voluntary alliance. The "semi-apes" of whom Hitler speaks with such loathing will be flying aeroplanes and manufacturing machine-guns. The Fascist dream of a slave empire will be at an end. On the other hand, if we are defeated we simply hand over our own victims to new masters who come fresh to the job and have not developed any scruples.

But more is involved than the fate of the coloured peoples. Two incompatible visions of life are fighting one another. "Between democracy and totalitarianism," says Mussolini, "there can be no compromise." The two creeds cannot even, for any length of time, live side by side. So long as democracy exists, even in its very imperfect English form, totalitarianism is in deadly danger. The whole English-speaking world is haunted by the idea of human equality, and though it would be simply a lie to say that either we or the Americans have ever acted up to our professions, still, the *idea* is there, and it is capable of one day becoming a reality. From the English-speaking culture, if it does not perish, a society of free and equal human beings will ultimately arise. But it is precisely the idea of human equality— the "Jewish" or "Judaeo-Christian" idea of equality—that Hitler came into the world to destroy. He has, heaven knows, said so often enough. The thought of a world in which black men would be as good as white men and Jews treated as human beings brings him the same horror and despair as the thought of endless slavery brings to us.

It is important to keep in mind how irreconcilable these two viewpoints are. Some time within the next year a pro-Hitler reaction within the left-wing intelligentsia is likely enough. There are premonitory signs of it already. Hitler's positive achievement appeals to the emptiness of these people, and, in the case of those with pacifist leanings, to their masochism. One knows in advance more or less what they will say. They will start by refusing to admit that British capitalism is evolving into something different, or that the defeat of Hitler can mean any more than a victory for the British and American millionaires. And from that they will proceed to argue that, after all, democracy is "just the same as" or "just as bad as" totalitarianism. There is *not much* freedom of speech in England; therefore there is *no more* than exists in Germany. To be on the dole is a horrible experience; therefore it is *no worse* to be in the torture-chambers of the Gestapo. In general, two blacks make a white, half a loaf is the same as no bread.

But in reality, whatever may be true about democracy and totalitarianism, it is not true that they are the same. It would not be true, even if British democracy were incapable of evolving beyond its present stage. The whole conception of the militarised continental state, with its secret police, its censored literature and its conscript labour, is utterly different from that of the loose maritime democracy, with its slums and unemployment, its strikes and party politics. It is the difference between land power and sea power, between cruelty and inefficiency, between lying and self-deception, between the SS man and the rent-collector. And in choosing between them one chooses not so much on the strength of what they now are as of what they are capable of becoming. But in a sense it is irrelevant whether democracy, at its higher or at its lowest, is "better" than totalitarianism. To decide that one would have to have access to absolute standards. The only question that matters is where one's real sympathies will lie when the pinch comes. The intellectuals who are so fond of balancing democracy against totalitarianism and "proving" that one is as bad as the other are simply frivolous people who have never been shoved up against realities. They show the same shallow misunderstanding of Fascism now, when they are beginning to flirt with it, as a year or two ago, when they were squealing against it. The question is not, "Can you make out a debating-society 'case' in favour of Hitler?" The question is, "Do you genuinely accept that case? Are you willing to submit to Hitler's rule? Do you want to see England conquered, or don't you?" It would be better to be sure on that point before frivolously siding with the enemy. For there is no such thing as neutrality in war; in practice one must help one side or the other.

When the pinch comes, no one bred in the western tradition can accept the Fascist vision of life. It is important to realise that now, and to grasp what it entails. With all its sloth, hypocrisy and injustice, the English speaking civilisation is the only large obstacle in Hitler's path. It is a living contradiction of all the "infallible" dogmas of Fascism. That is why all Fascist writers for years past have agreed that England's power must be destroyed. England must be "exterminated", must be "annihilated", must "cease to exist". Strategically it would be possible for this war to end with Hitler in secure possession of Europe, and with the British Empire intact and British sea-power barely affected. But ideologically it is not possible; were Hitler to make an offer along those lines, it could only be treacherously, with a view to conquering England indirectly or renewing the attack at some more favourable moment. England cannot possibly be allowed to remain as a sort of funnel through which deadly ideas from beyond the Atlantic flow into the police states of Europe. And turning it round to our own point of view, we see the vastness of the issue before us, the all-importance of preserving our democracy more or less as we have known it. But to *preserve* is always to *extend*. The choice before us is not so much between victory and defeat as between revolution and apathy. If the thing we are fighting for is altogether destroyed, it will have been destroyed partly by our own act.

It could happen that England could introduce the beginnings of Socialism, turn this war into a revolutionary war, and still be defeated. That is at any rate thinkable. But, terrible as it would be for anyone who is now adult, it would be far less deadly than the "compromise peace" which a few rich men and their hired liars are hoping for. The final ruin of England could only be accomplished by an English government acting under orders from Berlin. But that cannot happen if England has awakened beforehand. For in that case the defeat would be unmistakable, the struggle would continue, the *idea* would survive. The difference between going down fighting, and surrendering without a fight, is by no means a question of "honour" and schoolboy heroics. Hitler said once that to *accept* defeat destroys the soul of a nation. This sounds like a piece of claptrap, but it is strictly true. The defeat of 1870 did not lessen the world-influence of France. The Third Republic had more influence, intellectually, than the France of Napoleon III. But the sort of peace that Petain, Laval and Co have accepted can only be purchased by deliberately wiping out the national culture. The Vichy Government will enjoy a spurious independence only on condition that it destroys the distinctive marks of French culture: republicanism, secularism, respect for the intellect, absence of colour prejudice. We cannot be *utterly* defeated if we have made our revolution beforehand. We may see German troops marching down Whitehall, but another process, ultimately deadly to the German power-dream, will have been started.

The Spanish people were defeated, but the things they learned during those two and a half memorable years will one day come back upon the Spanish Fascists like a boomerang.

A piece of Shakespearean bombast was much quoted at the beginning of the war. Even Mr Chamberlain quoted it once, if my memory does not deceive me:

> *Come the four corners of the world in arms*
> *And we shall shock them: naught shall make us rue*
> *If England to herself do rest but true.*

It is right enough, if you interpret it rightly. But England has got to be true to herself. She is not being true to herself while the refugees who have sought our shores are penned up in concentration camps, and company directors work out subtle schemes to dodge their Excess Profits Tax. It is goodbye to the *Tatler* and the *Bystander,* and farewell to the lady in the Rolls-Royce car. The heirs of Nelson and of Cromwell are not in the House of Lords. They are in the fields and the streets, in the factories and the armed forces, in the four-ale bar and the suburban back garden; and at present they are still kept under by a generation of ghosts. Compared with the task of bringing the real England to the surface, even the winning of the war, necessary though it is, is secondary. By revolution we become more ourselves, not less. There is no question of stopping short, striking a compromise, salvaging "democracy", standing still. Nothing ever stands still. We must add to our heritage or lose it, we must grow greater or grow less, we must go forward or backward. I believe in England, and I believe that we shall go forward.

Printed in Great Britain
by Amazon

21692644R00058